Unwinding the Clock

Bodil Jönsson

Unwinding the Clock

Ten Thoughts on
Our Relationship to Time

Translated from the Swedish
by Tiina Nunnally

Harcourt, Inc.
New York   San Diego   London

www.harcourt.com

This is a translation of *Tio Tankar Om Tid*

Library of Congress Cataloging-in-Publication Data
Jönsson, Bodil.
[Tio tankar om tid. English]
Unwinding the clock: 10 thoughts on our relationship
to time/Bodil Jönsson; translated from the Swedish by
Tiina Nunnally.
p.   cm.
ISBN 0-15-100539-7
1. Time—Philosophy. 2. Time perception. 3. Time and space.
I. Title.
BD638 J66 2001
304.2'3—dc21   00-050566

Text set in Aldus
Designed by Linda Lockowitz

First U.S. edition
K   J   I   H   G   F   E   D   C   B   A

Printed in the United States of America

Contents

Please Read This First

I've been working with much of the contents of this book for more than twenty years. My thoughts have already been woven into numerous letters, conversations, articles, speeches, Swedish radio broadcasts, and books. Much can be found on the audiotape *A Different Kind of Wallet*, which Karin Örnfjäll and I recorded together in December 1997.

Now, by request, these thoughts have also become a book. "By request" may sound a little pretentious, but there has actually been strong interest. I'm not really surprised by this—having spent so many years on my own thoughts about time, I've come to realize that lots of other people have also been pondering their relationship to time. They want to discuss it, they want support for their own thoughts, and they want to exchange ideas. Not just to narrow it down but also so they can reflect on and perhaps even learn to deal successfully with time and its passage.

Time is not something you can resolve once and for all. You're probably going to have to do as I do: keep at it all your life, going up and down a staircase with four steps. To take the first step you have to start getting used to thoughts about time other than such depressing statements as "I just don't have enough time!," "There's no time!," or "I don't know how I'm going to find the time."

Standing on the first step, you begin to realize that you actually have more ways of relating to time than just narrowing it down. If you make it to the second step, it means that you've found some more methodical ways of thinking about your time and its usage. Maybe you recognize these thoughts, are able to structure them, make associations, and link them together. And you might even chuckle a little at yourself and wonder, "Am I back in that same spot again?" If you take another step up, you've learned to describe your thoughts about time and your way of living to the fullest in the midst of ongoing time. This step is important not only because you can discuss ideas with other people, but also because it greatly enhances your own thinking. Not until you conceptualize your thoughts can they serve as a basis for further thinking. Then you won't have to start from scratch every time. It's as if you could stand on your own shoulders. And maybe in this way you can crawl up to the fourth step, where you'll be able to compare your methods and idea systems with others that might also be possible.

On the fourth step you can pause for a bit and imagine that you've understood everything that's important for your relationship to time. But then a new event may arise, a new life situation may occur, or you'll merely (and most commonly!) fall back into old habits, and then it's all over with your stoic meditation from up above. You can start all over from step one, two, or three. Each time it will seem a little easier.

I'm not going to talk about these steps anymore in the book. It's just an internal image, and it might be appropriate only for myself. On the other hand, I *am* going to talk about things I've experienced and a lot of the thoughts I've had as I crawled up or down these stairs. It will make me happy if what I've written proves useful to you.

Writing this book has been a joyful experience. All of it. Making selections from previous materials, writing new sections, and then putting them all together in a new bouquet. And to top it all off, being able to date this book as I have below. Three ones and three nines are not any old sequence of numbers. It's a date just as extraordinary as a two followed by three zeroes.

Stenshuvud, 1/1/1999

Chapter One

Time–The Only
Thing You Have

I don't have many idols in my life. Maybe only one: my grandmother. She died before I turned seven, but she's the person who dominates the few distinct memories I have of my childhood.

No doubt there are many reasons for my strong memory of my grandmother, but right now I'm thinking of a specific one: she never had too little time. By our standards she had too little space, and certainly she sometimes had too little food, heat, and light. But she didn't have too little time. It never seemed that way to her; she didn't look at life that way.

Two generations later, I belong to a generation and a culture that think of themselves as having too little time. Too little of the only thing that a human being possesses.

The average human life span in Sweden lasts about 30,000 days. They are what make up our capital, our individual fortune. This is why it's not reasonable, or even appropriate, for us to accept our experience of time as something that is in short supply.

How did the relatively calm life of the 1950s— after a half-century rise in the material standard of living—become transformed into such apparent disquietude and what is perceived by many as disharmony? The most important reason might be that a human being's innate mental rhythms are adaptable and pliable to a degree that is actually detrimental. When creative people began surrounding themselves with more and more technology, they were forced to live a life in which they no longer controlled their own time. Human creativity, inventiveness, sensitivity, and flexibility have come up against technology's predictability, lack of imagination, and insensitivity to change. Or— to put it another way—the human being, who is characterized as forgetful, illogical, disorganized, and emotional, tries to coexist with technology, which has a good memory and is precise, logical, well organized, and consistently intractable.

The human being's inability to control time because of innate characteristics has never been seen before in the evolutionary process. When Leonardo da Vinci drew his famous picture of "man as the measure of all things," it was a *geometric* image. It wasn't necessary to think of anything other than distances, surface areas, volumes, and the relationships among them. Our era exhibits a need for a new image of man as the measure of all things. But that image hasn't yet been invented.

A Different Kind of Wallet

What do you own that can be transformed into money or human companionship? Or into interaction with your surroundings (the environment, nature, technology, products), or into something that can teach you to develop feelings and knowledge? You have your time, of course. Consider the familiar, old kind of wallet for holding money, with a slot for your dollar bills. Then imagine there's another slot for the people around you, for those closest to you and for the other people in your life. The third slot is for the rest of your surroundings, made up of the environment, nature, and work. Finally, there is a slot for what exists inside you: your thoughts and feelings.

Dividing things up in this way may at first seem uninteresting or pointless, since it isn't possible to move things from one slot to another. You can't buy knowledge with money, you can't replace human interaction with gadgets. But next to the wallet lies the symbol for the gold standard itself: time. Time can be moved to any of the slots. Time is the true capital.

Most often you're concerned with more than one slot at once, but it can still be instructive to try to separate them. You will then see that an astonishingly large share of both individual and communal efforts are placed in the money slot. What happens when we try to redistribute the emphasis among the four slots? Most important, what happens when we put more emphasis on time, which is the medium of exchange and is needed to make deposits and withdrawals? We may then be able to start considering seriously how to establish a Time Protection Agency, just as we now have an Environmental Protection Agency.

Missing the Crucial Linchpin

When the economy runs amok, when the ecological system falters, when the earth, air, and water suffer an unimaginable series of blows, and when no one actually sees more than a limited number of symptoms, then it's time to rethink things. What if we're missing the crucial linchpin? We failed to see the fundamental cause when the Three Mile Island nuclear reactor suddenly began showing alarming warning signs. The steps taken were all according to the rule book, and yet they were all wrong because they were based on cause-and-effect relations that had nothing to do with the actual situation. What happened was that a valve got stuck. Since no one realized this, however, the wrong measures were taken. Over and over again.

In a similar way, it might be bad for our environment, our social relationships, and our peace of mind if we don't come to grips with the crucial linchpin in this situation: namely, our relationship to time. What if it is stuck? And what if a different perception of time can steer us toward an attitude that is more friendly to the environment than any of the direct efforts we have made on its behalf?

Anything that leads us away from the "time is money" belief is good. As is any movement away from having *money* serve as the gold standard for life. In the past, the danger behind this idea was more obvious. Consider, for example, the wives of laborers who rebelled against union demands that their husbands be paid *with money* for their work, that is, for their time. Until then, payment had always been made in kind, and this was the linchpin of survival. The only money then existing in a household belonged to the women. If, in addition to milking ten to fifteen cows several times a day, women managed to do a little handiwork or something similar, they might earn a few coins for themselves. Pin money. This was important to them. But the thought that *all* work, even their husbands', could be compensated with money, the thought that time could be turned into money, was perceived as a genuine threat.

Much has happened since then, and a large part of Western development has revolved around "saving time." I can't resist giving another one of my favorite examples of how crazy things can get when we talk about saving time. Let's say that you have a thirty-mile commute to work, so you drive sixty miles a day. This takes you about an hour. But does it really take one hour to drive sixty miles? Let's do the arithmetic (the figures are already slightly outdated, but the ratios are correct). In Sweden it costs approximately 20 dollars to drive 60 miles. You have to work to earn those 20 dollars. The average wage per hour, after taxes, is 5 dollars. That means it takes four hours to earn the money for the commute. So it doesn't take one hour to drive sixty miles—it takes $1 + 4$ hours, or a total of five hours! Which results in an average speed of 12 miles per hour (60 miles in 5 hours). So you might as well ride your bike to work!

Time to Rethink Things?

It's a striking example. How could you turn it to your advantage? It's by no means easy to say to your boss: "I'm thinking of redistributing my time. Instead of an eight-hour work day plus a one-hour commute by car, I'm now going to work five hours and bicycle for four." A person's timetable is not self-contained and easily changed; rather, it's inter-connected with the business world, the workplace, the marketplace, the social welfare system, and the whole public sector. Almost everything is based on traveling by car. But that doesn't mean it's danger-ous or useless to think: "Maybe I could just as well ride my bike." For one thing, you can always change some small routine so that it suits you bet-ter. For another, big changes start out in exactly this way. With calculations, images, metaphors, and comparisons that help us laugh at the supposedly rational way we plan our lives.

In this same manner I could examine one area of our lives after another. Take a look, for instance, at the price of an average plane ticket and then think about whether you could just as well have gone by bike! Are we really in such a rush to get to a place that we can't get there any other way? Well, maybe sometimes. But things don't actually go as fast as we think they do. We pay for the time we purportedly gain, with the effort we put into our jobs in order to buy our saved time.

Whenever I meet someone who tells me about a newly purchased gadget that is supposed to save time, I ask—if I dare—"So what are you going to use that time for?" It's a good question, but a dangerous one. It points to the very linchpin: Here you are right now, and it feels as if time is slipping away from you, as if it's going faster and faster. What do you do? You buy something to save time. But time just goes faster, and so you buy something else to save even more time…

I was about thirty when I started thinking about this. I had three small children and an exciting job—and time was passing more quickly every day. I talked to a woman whom I then regarded as ancient—she was probably no more than fifty. When I rather hesitantly attempted to explain my problem to her, she said, "And you say that now, when you're so young! Just wait and see!"

Her words made a deep impression on me. I couldn't shake them! Because if there's one thing a scientist knows how to do, it's how to think logically. If it was true that the accelerating pace I had started to notice would only get worse—well, in that case my life would soon be over. And that's not what I had in mind at all, since I thought it was good to be alive.

Time Out

A seed was sown. In all secrecy I began a personal crusade to "stop time." I decided to take a strong measure: For a certain period I would do nothing at all instead of rushing around like a chicken with its head cut off. Well, "nothing" is a slight exaggeration. Since I couldn't change the way I was, I was still doing quite a bit.

After Christmas I took some time out from my job, almost two months (back then the expression "time out" hadn't gained widespread use outside the sports world). I wasn't sick or burned out or depressed; I just wanted to stop time. During the first week I cleaned the attic and started making preparations to polish the hardwood floor, but after awhile I settled down. I stayed home the whole time. That was important. Not to go away, not to do anything else, just to wait. And gradually my sense of eternal time came back. The panic about "What am I supposed to be doing? What am I forgetting?" and the anxiously murmured "But, but, but, empty, empty, empty—what now?" faded away little by little. When I look back, I see that time has never gone as fast for me as it did before that time out. I'm convinced that the trick would work again. If I ever again feel like a caged squirrel, I will just take another long time out and in that way return to a life that is in reasonable harmony with the flow of time.

I still use this old trick on a daily basis, but on a very small scale. Of course life seems to career around me too. And all too often. But I recognize this and can step back a bit, take a breath, and start over. In a different state of mind. Even when I'm stuck in the cage, it makes a big difference to know that I won't be caged forever. Sooner or later I'll get myself out of it.

Deep inside I now know that I don't have too little time. I have plenty of time. I know that this sort of reasoning provokes other people. Both friends and strangers have demonstrated this by their questions, which are usually mixed with fear. It's true that they ask me how it is that *I* have so much time, but I can't fail to notice that they're really asking about their own relationship to time.

Is it possible to have plenty of time? How is that done?

No Single Solution

There are a couple of sure-fire tricks. I'll get to them in a minute. But it's important to remember that this is not really an area conducive to the sort of quick fixes prevalent in many time-management contexts. Rather, it's a personal matter, impossible to take in unless you work through it deep inside yourself, at your very core, and then return to it time and again. To encourage such an approach, I'm writing this book in a kind of Krilon style. (The Krilon trilogy by the Swedish Nobel laureate Eyvind Johnson is an excellent analysis of the importance of conversation: conversation between people and conversation inside an individual.)

Like Krilon I will circle around the arguments, coming back to them again and again, from slightly different angles, touching on them in slightly different places. I do this partly because it's often the best way to learn—not through single events, and not through strict repetition either, but through variation. And partly because it's impossible to resolve your relationship with time once and for all.

But you *can* learn to recognize symptoms. You can learn some basic tricks that will help break the destructive spin of time. You can also learn to laugh at yourself a little. Laughter is always liberating.

Free Time

Whether you admit to the lifelong perception that you have too little time or whether you feel that you have plenty of time, a change in your consciousness about time will lead to new priorities in what you do and how you make use of time. The person with the jam-packed calendar is forced to see how all his notes and scribblings cancel each other out. How he has to prioritize over and over again, excluding things in order to get anything done. Excluding some things in order to allow for others. Arranging his life to allow for free time, so that he can think and do something new. This requires time and space, and the people around him must show greater consideration and stop interrupting him. And—above all—he must stop interrupting himself and letting details dominate his life.

Having lots of balls in the air doesn't mean that you have to juggle them all at once. Maybe you need to be uninterrupted while you catch them, one at a time. Later on they can occasionally be changed in quick succession, but you should never hold too many. The limit is different for everyone. I can handle an enormous number of balls, but as I add one more and then another, I reach a limit that is almost ridiculously obvious. If I go beyond it, I lose control and drop even the one last ball that I'm so maniacally trying to hold on to. A preliminary stage to this collapse is that the more balls I add, the longer it takes me to think and act.

To the Law of Multiplicity

Once upon a time I thought that getting older would be like moving down a narrowing funnel—life would just get more constricted and more regimented. From what I've had the chance to experience so far, it seems quite the opposite. Since no one told me anything about this when I was young, I'd like to attest to this here and now: life doesn't have to get worse as we age. It's even possible that experiences can become fuller with each day that passes. Perhaps it seems this way to me because I've experienced so much that each new event evokes numerous associations in my life. I couldn't have been aware of such multiplicity thirty years ago, simply because I didn't have enough experiences then. It's like the biologist who can distinguish hundreds of different kinds of grass while other people see only green and more green. Or the music connoisseur who can immerse himself in the whole composition or separate out the voices or maybe ponder over similarities to another piece of music. The experiences of experts are richer than those of other people. And that's why their next experience and the one after that will be even richer. The spiral moves in the right direction. Provided they don't become blasé, of course.

Like many others, over the years I've acquired a deep core of confidence. I dare to act, to feel, to sample, and to experience. This means that I push at boundaries just as much now as I did in the past. It's as if the funnel has been turned upside down, and life is expanding instead of contracting.

Sometimes I'm struck by how little I remember from those periods of my life when everything was going smoothly. I recall them as a mood, a shimmering happiness. That's a good thing, of course, but it's all I retain. What lives on in my memory, what has made a lasting impression on me, are those times that have been particularly difficult. This doesn't mean that I brood over problems or even that I dwell on injustices. I seem to possess the enviable ability to resist becoming bitter. No, it's because of what I've gained from difficulties that I'm almost always grateful for what I've been through. Difficulties have given me a capacity to experience more, to dare more, to want more, and they have given me a different relationship to time.

Alternating Activities

There are both advantages and disadvantages to alternating an activity with another activity or with a break, provided you can make it through the nonproductive and gnawing stress that may exist during the transition periods.

One advantage of alternating activities may be that it allows thoughts to develop at a slower pace. Maybe what we need sometimes is to be a little bored. We need to let a thought age a bit before it can be processed in those parts of ourselves deep inside, where we have no possibility of exercising control. You can't be constantly thinking up new ideas. You also need to take a break. And this break can be achieved either by stopping what you're doing or by doing something else.

One disadvantage of alternating activities may be that it takes a disproportionately long time to enter into or exit from an activity. When the start-up is long and the braking distance great, there's simply no room left for the activity itself. I'll write more about this under the heading "Setup Time" in chapter 3.

One advantage is that you're free from monotony.

One disadvantage may be that the multiplicity causes you to prioritize poorly, so that only the quick, easy, and ultimately unimportant things get done, not the things that are difficult, interesting, or relevant in the long term.

Standing Still and Moving

The abilities that emerge in a state of inertia are different from those that emerge in a state of motion. This applies to both human beings and inanimate objects. Just think about a bottle of syrup. What can you determine about the syrup if you don't tip the bottle? You can see its color, you can stick your finger inside, and you can taste it. But the fact that syrup moves slowly, to put it mildly, is something you won't know until you actually turn the bottle upside down, setting its contents in motion. That's when its dynamic properties emerge.

Dynamic properties are not revealed in the static state. Discovering the dynamic properties of an individual you've met before only in static situations is like meeting an entirely different person. The person who sits beside you in front of a campfire in the woods only partially resembles the person caught up in the rush of the big city.

It's not so strange that the desired qualities listed in help-wanted ads have changed. In the past it was trustworthiness and stability (static traits); nowadays creativity, sensitivity, and initiative are valued most.

Simultaneity

In the past, time was allowed to shepherd the passage of nature. Time was nature's marvelous way of preventing everything from happening all at once. Now it seems as if that property of time has been knocked out of play—(almost) everything happens at once. The magic boots that previously could differentiate what had lasting value from what was ephemeral by trudging day in and day out over all inventions, research results, and newfangled ideas have today lost their function. All our imaginings about how things will be in the long run may turn out to be irrelevant, because the long run may not be particularly far off after all.

Frightening? Yes, maybe. But it's also fabulous that I'm alive *now*, when everything around me is completely within my reach. Your time is not just the span of time you have; it's also the time you

have *right now*. Simultaneity is an important concept. Of course you haven't met all the people
you'd like to meet, but in principle there's nothing
to prevent you from doing so. But you can't talk
with people from the past or people living in the
future. The consequences of this are important on
a national scale as well. Today when one country
threatens another by, for instance, restricting its
neighbor's access to water, a conflict arises that
has to be resolved right now. But when a generation in one country today restricts the access to
water for a future generation in that same country or elsewhere, this lack of simultaneity means
that the conflict cannot be resolved right now. No
conversation can take place between the different
parties—between those who initiated the restric-
tion and those who will be subjected to it.

How Do You Know That Time Is the Only Thing You Have?

Time is felt most dramatically in connection with
the births or deaths of people you know. A tiny
new human being is suddenly alive, with all his
time ahead of him, and maybe in need of some of
your time too. Another person dies, and you can
no longer share time with her. Thoughts about
time (about the approximately 30,000 days we

possess) take on a lofty and existential quality. Or don't we dare think about it? A sense of not belonging may have a physical or social aspect, and yet there is also a feeling of rootlessness in time. But this feeling is often among the thoughts that are taboo.

Our daily lives are full of events, people, and places. Now and then we say that we're living in the moment, or at least we want to live in the moment. Completely. But the present can become paralyzed if you don't know what you're going to do in a month's time. It's necessary to have a vision of the future in order to live in the present. The same applies to the past and our access to memories. The past, present, and future are all cornerstones in the passage of our lives.

With this book I want to make it easier for you to discover the special nature of time, time as a unique phenomenon, even in the midst of daily life. The fact that "time is the only thing you have" can be experienced as a joy, an eye-opener, an exhortation or a challenge, all depending on your mood.

Chapter Two

Clock Time and Experienced Time

Everyone has internal scouts, scouts who are more or less active, depending on the circumstances. If you've just learned that you're pregnant, you'll see women with big bellies and parents with baby buggies everywhere. If you've started thinking that the spot on your back might be malignant, you'll feel it rubbing against your shirt all day long. If you're out hunting for mushrooms, the yellow birch leaves can be so easily mistaken for chanterelles. A person's perceptions are guided to a great extent by his scouts. Maybe we ought to see ourselves more as seekers than receptors of experience.

Sometimes knowledge can play a role in both

the type and intensity of the search and the experience. As it does, for example, for the biologist with regard to the multiplicity of species, or for the music connoisseur in the concert hall. Or for the astronomer who sees more in the night sky and looks at it differently than the amateur does.

How Many "Soons" Are There in a Quarter of an Hour?

It's a different story with time. We don't have many scouts keeping track of time inside us. You can't become a pro at experiencing time. You can learn to be punctual, you can study to be a watchmaker, you can become a logician and harmonize the whole flow of time, you can train yourself to be a project manager with the fantastic ability to squeeze in the time required for a specific assignment, or you can become a physicist and delve into the theoretical and experimental fundamentals of time. But when I sit here and ponder, "How long does a quarter of an hour last?" or "How many 'soons' are there in an hour?," being a physicist doesn't help a bit. Of course a physicist can explain better than most people how a second is defined and what fifteen minutes are, but that doesn't help me when I want to describe, using myself as the measuring device, the perceived duration of a quarter of an hour.

I think we'd better stick to two types of time and distinguish between them: *personal* (experienced) time and *clock* (actually atomic) time. The similarities between them are not particularly striking. We human beings aren't very good at registering objective clock time. Our built-in clocks run differently from day to day, from hour to hour, maybe even from minute to minute. In other words, they're not too reliable.

But experienced time is every bit as real as mechanized-atomic clock time—it's just that each is real in a different dimension. My personal time, my uniquely human perception of time, is something I can't share with anyone else, while the time information I need in order to meet with other people is the artificial measurement of time. How strange. But is it really?

No, it's not. Often the purpose of the technological, the artificial, is to enable us to excel at something that is *inter-human*. Some people say that technology is inhuman. That's not true. Individuals are the ones who are human or inhuman. Technology is technical, although occasionally it is simply inefficient. Its most common interaction with human beings is based on its inter-human capabilities. We wouldn't have invented telephones if there was no one to call; there wouldn't be any railroads if there was nowhere to travel. And there certainly wouldn't be any precision clocks if there weren't other people with whom we had to agree—on when to meet, for example, or how long to keep doing a specific activity.

Defined, Measurable Time: Clock Time

Describing artificial clock time is easier, because this is something on which human beings have agreed. Like other physical quantities, clock time is defined by its units. Nina Reistad and I once co-authored a book called *Experimental Physics,* in which we concluded, among other things, that it's no mystery that a second lasts precisely as long as it does, that a kilogram weighs what it does, or that a meter is exactly as long as it is. People simply chose the units to be a convenient size. The unit of time called a second is quite close to the time between two heartbeats. The unit of mass called a kilogram is also appropriate—a human being weighs a certain number of kilograms. The unit of length called a meter is suitable since we are one to two meters tall. The unit of temperature called one degree Celsius is appropriate because we are good at discerning temperature differences of one or two degrees.

But what do you have to do to make these units the same everywhere? Because this is what has actually happened over the years. Even people in places where meters, kilograms, and Celsius degrees are not commonly used still accept the measurements of 1 meter, 1 kilo, and 1°C. They can even convert their own units of measurement to these units. When it comes to time, it's worth noting that one second is the accepted unit everywhere.

Distance and Time

Wanting to make the units of distance and time immutable, people put their trust in things that could be observed everywhere and that were thought to last forever. That's why the units were linked to astronomical phenomena. In this way the length of one meter was defined as one tenmillionth of the distance along the surface of the earth from the equator to the North Pole. The concept of time and units of time were linked to astronomical movement. Gradually, however, as measuring technology was developed, it was discovered that heavenly phenomena are not at all immutable.

In 1870 the English physicist James Clerk Maxwell explained:

> If we want to obtain absolute, immutable units for length, time, and mass, we should not be dependent on the movement or mass of our planets but instead rely on the wavelength, frequency, and mass of imperishable, immutable, and completely identical atoms.

That's when rapid development occurred, leading to a definition of the meter based on atomic wavelengths and a definition of the second based on the frequencies of radiation from atoms and molecules. Since 1967, one second has been defined as the duration of 9,192,631,770 periods of the radiation that corresponds to the transition between two hyperfine levels in the basic state of the atom cesium 133.

But I don't know a single person who, by virtue of personal experience, could be persuaded to accept this definition. On the contrary, its strength lies in the fact that it's an objective definition independent of human beings. As a curiosity and provocative thought I'd also like to describe the definition of a meter, because nowadays—ever since Thursday, October 20, 1983—it is directly linked to the definition of a second. One meter is defined as the distance that light travels in a vacuum during the time 1/299,792,458 of a second.

Length, in other words, is now defined not as length but as something based on time. This is a result of the strange situation that arose in the 1970s. Back then, for the first time, the speed of light could be measured in a vacuum, expressed in meters per second, more precisely than the unit of one meter was defined! It was ridiculous, and so the meter was redefined and directly linked to the second, as explained above.

In this way clock time and its defined world have taken on at least one trait in common with our contemporary experienced world: the calculations are made in terms not of distance but of time.

Personal, Experienced Time

You cannot affect physical time, clock time, and its definition or its passage. You can choose an ordinary mechanical clock and, like Gösta Ekstrof, exclaim:

> I don't want to have
> one of those digital miracles

that measure out my consumption of time
I want to keep
my global oracle
that lets me keep my illusion of immortality

But you won't change the fact that humanity has made it a point of honor to define units of time in a fashion that is independent of people, first in the cosmic world and now in the atomic microcosm.

Personal time, on the other hand, is your own. Both in terms of how you handle it and how you experience it in your thoughts and through your feelings. It's the personal, experienced time that we'll have for a very long time, maybe even forever. But it's clock time that we pursue. We render it more "effective." We divide it up into smaller pieces. And then we buy new technology in order to "save time." Most of these efforts are counterproductive if you want to have plenty of experienced time.

Infringements on Time Experiences

Experienced or personal time is the most important kind for the individual. Some environments are more conducive than others in terms of permitting the experience of personal time, of your own rhythm. In the past, trains were perfect moving sanctuaries. You had, of course, your departure time and your arrival time expressed in clock time, but in between you were free to experience time in your own unique way. On a train there were often fewer interruptions than in most other places.

Then this free zone was yanked away from those of us who loved trains. That's when the cell-phone junkies made their appearance, with all their chatter about balance sheets, Uncle Kalle's funeral, the results of their driving test, and the complications of Eva's whooping cough. But I don't want to know about any of these things. I want to be left in peace in my soundproof room. I refuse to accept other people intruding so unnecessarily on my personal time with their excitable conversation in the middle of my train compartment. Often loud and never natural. It's not natural to hear only half a conversation. In fact, it's so unnatural that you can't even block out the disruption, the way you usually can with normal background noises that are produced by conversations between your fellow travelers.

"Dear Swedish Railway," I wrote in 1995. "I would love to continue traveling by train. I suggest that you reserve a special compartment for the cell-phone junkies, where they can keep on slicing up time. Then the rest of us can continue to have our part of the train as a free zone. By the way, I think that lots of these cell-phone marauders will end up wanting to join us in the cell-phone-free area—the way smokers sit in the nonsmoking compartments when they're not actually smoking. Because once you've had a whiff of what experienced time can be, you won't give up trying to protect it."

And now at last they exist, these cell-phone-free compartments, safeguarded oases. Maybe trains can once again develop into environments where a sense of experienced time is strengthened and expanded.

Time Thinks

While I was inventing my concept of clock time versus experienced time here in Sweden, the rest of the world had apparently not given up pondering the same question. You can almost always be sure that if you happen to come up with a completely new idea, there will be one or more people sitting somewhere else in the world who at the exact same moment come up with the exact same idea. Maybe formulated in a slightly different way, but basically the same. "Time thinks," as Kristina Persson, the county governor of Jämtland, often says.

All the same, I was surprised when it turned out that I wasn't alone in my thoughts about clock time and experienced time. In 1990 the German philosopher Peter Heintel founded Tempus, "an organization to stretch out (delay, protract) time" (*Verein zur Verzögerung der Zeit*). This was not a joke (although the organization is marked by a great deal of humor), and Tempus now has a thousand members in Austria, Germany, Sweden, Italy, and Switzerland. Every year since 1991, they have organized seminars on the subject of time. The members are invited to present concrete examples of measures taken by themselves or others to handle personal time. They produce and sell publications, illustrations, and documentations on video.

I didn't find out about Tempus until a few years back, when I read about it in a Swedish newspaper. I sought out the organization's publications, and with eyes as big as saucers I sat there and read about Chronos (an exact copy of my "clock time") and Kairos (also a copy of my concept of "experienced time"). One of the Tempus books, *Zeitzeichen* (Signs of the Times), is promoted as a book for people who have everything—except time.

The organization is apparently an informal one, but it does produce quite a number of printed materials. Allow me to cite a few examples from the organization's texts:

"Speed up your life, and it will be over a lot quicker!"

"I have time—therefore I am."

"No matter how often you check on the olives, they won't ripen any faster."

Maybe it's not so strange that Tempus and I think alike, and that it's happening now. It's only in our era, so far removed from the struggle to eke out a daily subsistence, that such thoughts can arise. We now have time to think about time. And we need that time if we're going to get away from the clock fixation of industrialization and the attitude that "time is money."

How to Gain More Experienced Time

One major reason that you may be reading this book is that you're looking for an answer to the question "How do I gain more experienced time?" The first thing I can tell you is that you have to start making experienced time into a conscious notion inside yourself. Realize that the clock doesn't tell you everything—that it's not the one and only means of measuring time.

Once you have a firmly established idea of the nature of experienced time, you can start working on gleaning more from it. There are great opportunities for affecting your time if you learn to handle your setup time (chapter 3) in a respectful and conscientious way. And if you can find a balance between time that is divided up and time that is not (chapter 4).

Chapter Three

Setup Time

In order to concentrate, you need to be without interruptions. Without interruptions even from yourself. As you continue reading this, think about the number 478 and subtract 7 from it, then take 14 away from 471, 28 from 443, and so on. Yes, I really mean it: try to work through this simple subtraction exercise while you continue to read!

There aren't many things that we can do simultaneously. Some people have to stop what they're doing to chew gum. I'm very aware that I slow down as I'm running or pedaling my bike if I start thinking about something. We women are known for our ability to juggle lots of balls at the same time. Of course we can do this (and I know plenty of men who can too), but not just any old balls or any number of balls. (By the way, how far did you get with your subtraction? Did you even get as far as 400? Did you notice that I made a mistake with 471 minus 14? We're not meant to do these kinds of activities simultaneously.)

Some things can be done much better not only without interruptions but also after a certain *setup time*. Setup time—that's the time it takes to put things in order, to arrange things so that you can start on a specific task. For the lumberjack in the past, it was the time it took to hitch the horse to the log sledge. In factories, it's the time it takes to set up the machines. In the kitchen it's the clock time spent doing *mis-en-place,* which means doing the prep work before you can start cooking. Even in modern project planning a concept exists for the total amount of time it takes to get the process started.

This chapter deals with the idea of learning to recognize the different amounts of setup time required for different tasks. I'll also discuss how you can safeguard the investments you make in setup time. Setup time is not something that you want to waste—just as out in the country you never walked away from a harnessed horse without doing some forestry work. Or in the kitchen, where you never do the prep work unless you're actually going to cook the food. In exactly the same way, you should make use of the setup time invested in focusing your thoughts. You should guard it zealously and never let it go up in smoke because of some disturbance, such as a phone conversation.

Different Tasks, Different Setup Times

Sometimes it's a good idea to divide up your activities by type. I know that at first glance there may not seem to be any immediately discernible differences in setup times if I divide the tasks into the following categories:

Easy and fun	Easy and boring
Difficult and fun	Difficult and boring

But the difference in setup time is significantly greater than you may think. If you're confronted with tasks from all four categories, it's tempting to start with some of the "easy" ones. For them, the setup time is almost nothing. And most of us often feel pressured (by ourselves and by others) to get the "easy and boring" tasks out of the way so that we'll have more peace of mind to devote to the rest.

Everything would be fine if we had unlimited time, but the result of the process described above is that we usually don't even get to the difficult tasks. Only the nice, easy things get done. Not because the difficult tasks are less important to us and are thus given lower priority, or even because they're impossible to do. No, it's because we can't make it through the seemingly unproductive setup time preceding them.

I don't think this really has to do with performance anxiety. It's more like "setup time anxiety." If you just persevere during the setup time, the rewards for performance can be significantly greater for one big task than for many small ones. But it takes a strong sense of awareness to prioritize and then make it through the setup time required for a difficult task. Not to mention the fact that, faced with incomprehension from those around you, you must endure the growing pile of trivial matters. Setup time—how can you make others understand that this is setup time preceding some major task? How should you view it yourself?

Setup Time and Accessibility

Sometimes I think that I'm in the midst of setup time without even knowing it myself. It might manifest itself like this: something major is approaching its deadline (in Skåne we say it's "approaching the gallows"). I know that I should have started on it long ago. But instead it seems as if I've just been getting less and less productive, shifting down into low gear and devoting myself to all kinds of trivial matters—even though this isn't my intention. I wash the dishes and clean house and sew on buttons and poke around in the garden. Not until the last possible moment (and preferably even a little later than that) do I tackle the project. And can you believe that I get it done? As if by a miracle! One more time. But I no longer believe that the task was actually completed at the last minute—I think that all my inner resources were on the job. That's why my conscious self had to work slowly and do only simple tasks—my real thinking was taking place inside. Then, when it was time, there wasn't much left for my "self" to do.

Intellectual concentration requires its own kind of setup time—it may take hours, days, weeks, even months. When you have this time, you shouldn't squander it, of course. You need to stay in it. Make yourself inaccessible. Take a firm stand against the high priority given today to being constantly accessible, for example via cell phones.

It was more than fifteen years ago that I began evaluating my relationship to the telephone. I started with my phone at work. What could I do to make it shut up? I could punch the button that said I was in a meeting or on a business trip or at lunch, that I was teaching or had left for the day. But there was no button saying that I was taking care of my primary task, which was *to think* (in silence, on a piece of paper, using the computer, in the laboratory, or in conversation with my colleagues and students). I talked to some of the switchboard operators, and their reaction was that a caller would get angry if they said, "No, you can't talk to Bodil Jönsson right now—she's thinking!" The caller, according to the operators (and I think they're right), would say indignantly that if I wasn't doing anything more important than thinking, I could just as well answer the phone. But I didn't feel that way.

Dare to Be a Hermit

I've now learned that seclusion is so important both for my work and for myself that periodically I have to insist on living the life of a hermit. The fact that I always try to be present wherever I am is also important for the people I work with. They can be assured that I'm really *there* when we're together. No phones are allowed to interrupt us. If your job is to think, it's not acceptable to give in to your imagined or real obligations, or to irrelevant values. It's actually your own fault if routine research and routine training take the upper hand.

The setup time for thinking can vary greatly, depending on the kind of environment you find yourself in. For example, the constant and quick access to the Internet has affected my setup time for thinking. It has probably also affected my subconscious. I allow myself many more thought links now because I know that I can quickly and easily search for information related to what I'm thinking. There's a big difference between this possibility for actively searching *in many directions* and the laconic information found in reference books.

Besides, reference books have their own setup time and bear the stamp of their era to a considerable extent. Because of the setup time they require, they seldom reflect contemporary thought patterns or breakthroughs—they essentially adhere to what has already been established, that is, to what is at least partially obsolete. No doubt this is necessary, so that recent events don't transform the reference work into something ephemeral.

My strongest example of how dated a reference work can be comes from a ten-year-old girl. For a school assignment about Liberia she wrote:

"The country is inhabited by savage and half-savage Negroes." I was astonished, to say the least, and when I asked her where she found such information, she replied, "That's what it said in the reference book." This "reference book" was *Lexicon of Our Time,* from 1938. Seldom has the title of a reference work been so ironic.

Youth as Setup Time for Life?

Let's move on to bigger things: thoughts about childhood and youth. Strangely enough, many people regard their childhood and youth as setup times for what will come later.

First a tiny example. Early on, you're taught not to bang your spoon on your plate so that later you'll have good table manners. That this training is relatively unimportant—except for the nerves of the parents at the time—is demonstrated by the fact that there isn't a single adult who sits around banging his spoon on his plate. Even though everyone has probably been given varying degrees of training. It's undoubtedly the same with spoon banging as with so many other things: it will pass on its own, if you just wait long enough.

If I move from table etiquette to life etiquette, I find the same attitude. Children and teenagers have to be trained so they'll be able to manage as adults—after a youth that is culturally determined and completely different from the biological one. It meant one thing to become an adult in a hunting society, something else in a farming society, and then again something altogether different in an industrialized society. The period of youth has been gradually extended so that individuals can acquire the skills demanded of adults by their era.

What happens if we no longer can manage to become adults? What would it mean if the younger generation of the 1990s turned out to be the first generation faced with the fact that adulthood doesn't seem to exist? Then it would become even more apparent that the most important parts of life—childhood and youth—should be given some intrinsic value in the present rather than merely a setup-time value for the future. My parents' generation had a distinct adulthood. If at the age of thirty-five my parents dressed the way they did at twelve, or if they ran around as if they were playing (nowadays it's called "jogging"), they would not have been accepted by their peers. An adult had to be an adult and behave like one. A child had to be a child, preferably invisible, and above all work on

42

becoming an adult someday. Or, as it says in the first four lines of a song:

> Someday I'll be a grownup
> and sensible like Mother and Father.
> But in my heart I'll always be a child,
> for the child belongs to God's kingdom.

What was it in the past that gave the older generation the upper hand? For one thing, the older generation had skills that younger people obviously needed. While adults taught youths the essentials of life, such as how to build a house, how to cook, etc., they also had a perfect opportunity for indoctrinating their children with the ideas of the older generation about such things as religion and morals. Today the situation is completely different. The want ads in the paper often ask for skills that the thirty-five-year-old parents are totally lacking, while the fifteen-year-old child learned them by playing games on the computer. Then it's not easy to claim that "age equals knowledge" and that the young should use their time as setup time.

When it comes to our era, those of us who are older have no more experience than the young do. We actually have less, since we're locked into old ways of thinking, and for that reason we're more limited in what we can experience. Although experiences don't have to diminish in power just because we get older (as I wrote in chapter 1), thought patterns differ from one generation to another. A way of thinking that marks one generation will be completely different from the pattern that fundamentally affects the next.

Young Thinkologists Wanted

Young people, above all, are the ones needed to be thinkologists (just as much as they're needed as technologists). In the distribution of responsibility that should prevail between generations, I think the biggest responsibility of the younger generation should be to develop new ways of thinking, and to show what happens when you start off with a completely new premise. To discover new patterns for human respect and human activities, we adults need help from those who have never been part of the formal "define-your-relevance-through-your-work" era. It's when we view new experiences from the perspective of old ways of thinking that the experiences become distorted—almost the way things look in a house of mirrors at an amusement park. Undoubtedly part of this distortion is our existing "house of thoughts" about unemployment—that work has suddenly become a sought-after, scarce commodity that entices more and more outsiders. How did such an idea arise in the first place?

Work is certainly not an ancient human dream—on the contrary. For instance, I've never seen a single picture of paradise in which the people are doing anything but lying around.

As far as I can tell, the present particular type of work shortage—the shortage of work in the formal sense—isn't merely going to continue, it's going to increase. On the other hand, there's no shortage of work in the real sense of the word. That's one reason it's important for a strong group of young, clear-thinking individuals to help institute different ways of thinking about unemployment vs. the actual content of life. After all, there's a lot that people want to do, and a lot that needs to be done.

In the classic Hans Christian Andersen fairy tale "The Emperor's New Clothes," it was a child who spoke the truth. I still believe that very young children are the best truth tellers, but so many adults refuse to take children seriously. Teenagers and young people in their twenties, however, are given respect because of their height, their voting powers, their skills, or their accomplishments, such as in the computer world, which has suddenly become so crucial to everyone. While the adults are reading newspapers and maybe wondering whether their neighborhood should remain rural or become a developed community, the kids are already part of the World Wide Web community.

Ancient Old Boys and Nonexistent Youths

One of the much-cherished pictures I use to prod my thoughts is a photo of the negotiation table at the Rio Conference (the United Nations conference on the environment in 1992). Half the people in the picture belong to the category "old boys." I usually think of this photo in terms not of women vs. men, but rather of old vs. young. Despite the fact that it won't be long before half the world's population is eighteen or younger, the control of the world's future is in the hands of very old men. It's not reasonable to expect that this pervasive domination by the older generation will continue much longer.

I have another picture with a UN connection in my postcard collection. It's a photo of the hall where the Security Council meets. In this one you can't see how old the delegates are, since there isn't a single person in the picture. The table, chairs, and room speak for themselves. "No matter what," the picture says to me, "people have always tried." They've tried to mediate, tried to persuade each other, tried to arrive at compromises and new possibilities.

It will be exciting to watch as the young take power. But maybe it won't be power in formal democracies on a local or global level that they will want to assume. Maybe they'll find completely new forms of power. Under any circumstances, it's important that they don't perceive their youth as a training period, a setup time for later adulthood. There's too much in the ledger of our era that points in the wrong direction (the environment, war, growing gaps between the rich and the poor, the inability of democracy to handle the economy, etc.). We need new ways of thinking and acting. I hope young people realize that they don't have to be like the adults of today.

Summary

In terms of setup time—just as with experienced time—you have to start by allowing the concept to sink in. Then you can try to analyze how an altered view of setup time might make it possible for you to act differently.

I've taken examples from several different perspectives:

- how different setup times for easy and difficult tasks strongly affect the distribution of what gets done
- how the setup time for a major task can sometimes manifest itself as a period of evasions
- how the environment, such as easy access to information via the Internet, can influence our setup time
- how youth is often considered to be a setup time for adult life

Chapter Four

Divided and
Undivided Time

After I made my one-time effort to stop time, I decided to change my lifelong perception. I argued: "If I can fool myself into thinking that I don't have enough time, couldn't I just as well fool myself into thinking that I have plenty of time?" So I decided to have plenty of time. I didn't try to give up all relation to time. I don't think that would be possible in our time-fixated culture. You have to decide either that you have plenty of time or that you don't have enough time—there's no middle ground.

But can I really experience what it's like to have plenty of time? Yes, I can. Plenty-of-time joy is no more wrong than the not-enough-time nightmare. It's easy to change your attitude—in principle. On the other hand, it may be difficult to break the habit of feeling panicked about the passage of time. But once you've done that, time can become a gold mine—a significantly more pleasant image than time as a rivulet that is constantly drying up.

See for yourself whether my lifelong perception (having plenty of time) will work for you too. The fact is that when I started telling myself that I had plenty of time, and even said it out loud, I actually began to have more time. Occasionally I backslide and get turned around, but I'm always aware that soon I'll take a deep breath and re-establish the proper order. The order in which there is plenty of time. This doesn't mean that I do little. I actually do too much. But by using two rules I can keep the feeling alive that time is endless. The first rule has to do with safeguarding my setup time, by taking it into consideration in advance and by planning for it. And by having respect for it and its torments. The second rule has to do with not dividing my life into too many small pieces. What was it, for example, that made my childhood summers seem endless? Well, my summers weren't divided up. I didn't have to go to handball camp before midsummer, to Mallorca the first week of July, to visit my grandmother on

July 15, to scout camp on July 22, and to visit my other grandmother the first week of August. If you do all these things, no interval will be longer than a week. And one week, as everyone knows, doesn't last forever. A week is finite. It's not possible to put together eight finite weeks and end up with a summer that's endless. A summer has to be undivided to give the feeling of endlessness.

Connected blocks of time give you space in time. Space to be in. Timeless space. This is the direct opposite of the school timetable, which obstructs opportunities for learning. The school timetable doesn't respect the students' setup time and constantly breaks their concentration. For more on this, see chapter 5, "TTT—Thoughts Take Time."

A New Redistribution

Open your pocket calendar and take a look at how segmented your time is. Think about what would happen if you carried out a redistribution of time ownership comparable to the great redistribution of land ownership in Sweden in the eighteenth century. I don't think any other cultural-geographical change in Sweden made such a great change in people's lives as the land redistribution did. Today we're being challenged individually and collectively to carry out instead a redistribution of time ownership. If we meet this challenge, it will mean profoundly positive changes for many of us at the very core of our lives.

Picture a map of the Swedish countryside before and after the land redistribution. For the most part, the change didn't mean that people ended up with more or fewer acres, it meant greater value, because the fields were joined to make larger units. It's the same thing with time. Undivided time is for many of us much more valuable than time divided up. The difference is so great that both types of time really shouldn't be measured in the same way, with hours of the clock. Divided and undivided time are at least as different as a squirrel is from a hedgehog. Counting "pieces" is actually quite meaningless. It's true that most train schedules from Lund to Stockholm show a travel time that is significantly longer than the trip by plane (although the fastest trains are starting to come close to the flying time if you count driving to and from the airport). But a train trip in a cell-phone-free compartment provides undivided, uninterrupted time for three to five hours, while the plane's three divided-up hours mean a direct loss of three undivided hours. Interruptions arise not only because of connecting flights, long lines, and boarding and deplaning but also because of announcements on the loudspeakers during the flight. I just want to be left in peace. Or talk to my neighbor without interruptions.

Conversations should take place in disturbance-free zones. Concentrated, inspired conversation is a widely undervalued source of new knowledge, new feelings, new impulses. There is so much inside each individual, so much that can be used to inspire and enrich others. But also the midwifery of thoughts—giving each other liberating impulses—takes time, and liberations of thought, when interrupted, are frequently wasted.

We often sit down in front of the TV to relax. Some people detest the way commercials break the programs up into pieces, and they seek refuge in stations without commercials. Without much luck, unfortunately, because on those stations the film previews are just as disruptive as the commercials. Who can stand it? Who wants to be tossed back and forth between announcements for completely different programs that will be shown several weeks in the future? What's happened to our relaxation?

One Possible Individual Development

Here's one view of the path toward less divided time:

- Explain to yourself that there really is a difference between divided and undivided time. If you don't understand the difference, you can't change the balance between the two.
- Stop thinking about divided and undivided time as measured with the same kind of hours.
- Try to achieve an individual redistribution in your own use of time.
- Try to achieve a common redistribution of how time is used within the communities you belong to.
- Examine your free time and work time, your plans for summer vacation, your school timetable, trips, leisure activities, TV viewing, etc., in terms of how much divided time vs. undivided time each contains. Then make a conscious choice based on how they affect the division of your time.

Advantages of Divided Time

Now let me make a 180° turn in the direction of this chapter and speak on behalf of those people who *look for* time divisions as a structure for their lives. There are lots of people who *need* to divide up their time in order to make sense of the world around them. Children want to know how many "soons" there are in an hour, and they need explanations such as "It's about as fast as half a cartoon show." Some adults also need the security of defining time in order to be able to experience any change at all. For them, timelessness is not some dream condition to strive for.

Let me illustrate this with Henry. When we first met, he almost never said a word. He would respond with a "Hi" if you said "Hi" to him, and he had a small stock of standard words and phrases, maybe a hundred, which he used sparingly, mumbling. After he got an Isaac personal electronic assistant, digital pictures entered Henry's life. It didn't matter much that they were digital—the important thing was that there were lots of them, and that they all had something to do with him personally. At first Henry couldn't use them unless they were printed out. But when printed out pictures were put up all over the walls, Henry began to change.

Suddenly he would stand in front of the pictures, attentive and focused. If you went over and stood next to him (which he didn't mind at all), you could hear that he was standing there mumbling. He seemed to be talking to the pictures. One day, as I was standing next to him, I was struck by an idea that has never left me: what was happening to Henry in front of the pictures was that *time* had entered his life. I think that previously it was very likely that Henry's life was not only nearly devoid of words—it was also nearly devoid of internal images. Quite simply, he had very few tools to use for thinking. If you have no words or pictures, there's nothing to hang your thoughts or memories on. This meant that Henry's previous existence had consisted only of a "present moment," followed by another "present moment," and so on. He couldn't mull things over, or wish for something, or anticipate anything—he could only (possibly) recognize himself through repetition. Experience doesn't go far without thoughts.

And so it was entirely reasonable that Henry could hardly learn anything before. Learning is based on variation, and variation in turn presupposes that something already exists: a memory, a point of reference that can be varied. It's sometimes said that "Repetition is the mother of learning," but that's not an absolute truth. Repetition can help us keep our focus, giving us fixed points that we can start from. But changes must be experienced in order to learn something. Variation is the mother of all learning.

For Henry, both repetition and variation were impossible before. He simply retained no active memory of anything he had participated in. But when he was given pictures, lots of pictures, of events he had personally experienced, all of a sudden the past became part of the present. The photos of past events brought inner pictures to life within Henry. Of course they were there before, as stored passive images, but they couldn't be activated. Now they took their place alongside the day's events. Afterward, it didn't take long before Henry started wishing for tomorrow.

And with that, an explosive period of learning began. Henry is over fifty years old. The first thing people noticed of Henry's inner revolution was his increased alertness. Then came an explosion of speech. It wasn't just a matter of a tremendous increase in Henry's vocabulary—it has also become a supremely active vocabulary. From the outside, Henry's explosive development is noticeable only in the way he uses the digital images. But inside him, it's likely that a consciousness of time has formed.

What gives the present its center is the fact that yesterday and tomorrow exist in today. What makes memories meaningful is the fact that there is a before and an after, a sense of order without which life would be chaos. Conciseness and mileposts must exist: that happened before we moved, that was after he shaved off his beard, and so on.

One group that I think would benefit greatly from dividing up and fixing time would be people who are slipping into senile dementia. It's during that period of life when memory functions are noticeably failing that we also, unfortunately, give up taking pictures. In other periods of our lives photos contribute to our ability to look back in time. When we were babies, our time was documented day by day, sometimes even hour by hour. But the older we get, the sparser the photo documentation. After we reach our fifties or sixties or seventies, it's rare that we have any photos of what we did yesterday or in the past few weeks.

What if we set up a system for photographing (digitally, of course) and displaying pictures on TV, so that we created our own "Sweet Memory Channel"? There would be pictures from long ago as well as the recent past. Starting and ending the day with a conversation, using pictures, about what we did today and yesterday and what we will do tomorrow should delay or decrease the tendency of memories to disintegrate or disappear.

Age Equals Knowledge

It's not just our own use of time but also the way others use time that can arouse the strangest feelings. In her essay "Age Equals Knowledge," Britt

Östlund describes how we sometimes misinter-
pret the solitude of old people. We have a guilty
conscience because we're not with our older fam-
ily members or friends, we try to visit them more
often, etc. Östlund writes in her essay that many
old people actually don't want lots of visits. They
want their solitude, their peace and quiet to think
about their lives. But it's not considered legitimate
simply to sit and think. That's why TV has become such a good excuse in their lives. They turn
on the TV, sink into a semidoze, and mull over
their own thoughts as they watch. And no one
says, "Aren't you listening?" or demands their attention. One of the conclusions of this essay is
that for many old people reflecting on their lives,
the television set may actually be a better non-
scrutinizing, nonjudgmental companion than any
of their fellow human beings are. From this point
of view, then, TV can be a good way in which to
have undivided experienced time.

The Undivided Law One More Time

Some people benefit from being able to divide
up their time: to put it into sections, structure it,
and gain an overview. The rest of us—people in
the midst of life—shouldn't assume that our wish
to have undivided time is the right thing for

everybody. Life as a flow without end can be a nightmare.

But even for people with memory problems, dividing time into pieces may not be wholly positive. That's because some of these individuals also have difficulty switching activities. The act of switching can take so much time that they never manage to experience the activity itself. The setup time, the shifting-gears time, then becomes the only time that exists, and this may also increase their confusion.

Maybe that's how you're feeling right now. You're being led into one way of thinking, and just as you begin to absorb it, I turn everything upside down and start looking at things from another perspective. But that's the way life is and always will be. Multifaceted. Not necessarily complicated, but certainly complex.

The Complex vs. the Complicated

Things that are complicated or difficult are what I usually take great pleasure trying to figure out and then occasionally present in a simpler form. At times something that is complicated is so inherently difficult that all simplifications end up being mostly stories or metaphors. But at other times something that is complicated, rather like a tangled skein of yarn, can be straightened out so that you can find the end of the string. And of course it's great if you can replace an unusable skein with a neatly shaped ball of yarn. The same holds true for skeins and balls of thought. You should simplify something that's complicated if you can, because then it becomes usable.

Time and our attitude toward time are not *complicated*. Instead, they're *complex*. If you try to simplify something that's complex, you're making a rash assumption. Damaging what's complex with the intention of simplifying it corrupts its core and destroys its existence. If something complicated can be compared to tangled yarn that can be straightened out, then something complex can be compared to a weaving. If you pull threads from a weaving, you ruin both its pattern and its form. It's the same way with time. Only respect for its complexity will get you anywhere. Simplifications aren't worth the trouble. With something complex you have to sneak up on it, twist and turn it, and look at it from different angles. My initial comparison to Krilon also applies here. And to all the examples I cite in the next chapter you can add this entire book: it takes time to think about time.

Chapter Five

TTT–Thoughts Take Time

Somewhere I've written
so each day I will see
the admonishing letters
TTT.

When you see how hard it is
to scrub off the grime,
don't ever forget that
Things Take Time.

PIET HEIN

The author and homegrown philosopher Piet Hein once coined the phrase TTT: Things Take Time. I myself say that thoughts take time. Thoughts take time when we're creating them, thoughts take time to keep (it might be called Thought Preservation), and it takes time to get rid of them after they've become outdated.

Thoughts even take time on a small scale. For instance, why is it that we still have to press two keys at once to make the "@" symbol? In this computer age of lightning-fast changes in technology, the idea that the "@" symbol should take only one tap of a key on a standard keyboard hasn't yet reached the designers.

Thoughts take even more time on a large scale. The greatest consumption of time is needed when we have to construct, rebuild, or demolish entire idea systems, entire idea infrastructures. Nothing rules the future as recklessly as an infrastructure of old ideas. That's why it's primarily through changes in the way we think that the future is affected.

For instance, we'll soon have to reassess the thought patterns of industrialization. They taught us that work is important, and that work is what we do on the job. To be "needed" became synonymous with having a job. We had free time for having fun or for tending to personal matters, such as taking care of our children or our aging parents, cooking, cleaning, and washing our shirts.

In the postindustrial age we will have to reassess this kind of thinking. But this means being able to survive bucking the trend. All trend breakers have at least one thing in common: they arouse strong feelings. Think about how it was when society decided to stop rewarding the drainage and reclamation of land in favor of the (re)creation of wetlands. Many people who had toiled to drain the land to make it arable reacted with anger and feelings of guilt. And understandably so. Just as predictable is the gale-force combination of fear and anger that will arise if and when we break with some of the impossible trends of our era and, for instance, (re)create a freedom from cars, although in a new form. And yet I think that's nothing compared to what we and our fellow citizens will face in creating a new definition of a "useful" member of society.

The Need to Be Needed

Of course we know that an individual can be needed in many different ways. Even when we're having fun, we like to know that we're needed. Maybe there's something that is inherently part of us—which we can find in most cultures across the ages—that makes us want to paint ourselves and dance when we don't have to work. To dance not only for our own sake but for the sake of the party, for the sake of the gods and the powers that be. Now don't take all this too literally. (Today painting yourself may stand for something other than putting on makeup; dancing may be something other than what we usually call dancing; and the gods and the powers that be may have nothing to do with religion.) The painting, the dancing, the gods, and the powers that be are symbols for the human need to express ourselves, and to do it together with other people. But we can't do things together if our thought assumptions do not agree.

Information technology (IT) is helping us become increasingly more individualistic and live in increasingly different worlds. But how do we enhance what we have in common? We share a cultural inheritance, but do we share any kind of cultural vision? I don't think so. I actually think that today we're experiencing a lack of any communal striving or, quite simply, any communal belief.

It's not easy to say how we should build such a vision. I can sympathize with the three-year-old who, upon answering the phone and saying, "Hello!," was asked, "Don't you have anything else to say?" He replied, "I already said hello, what else is there to say?" There's good logic in this kind of reasoning on the three-year-old level. But surely it can't be true that we've all become so individualistic that there's nothing else to say about our common future.

All These Manias

There's something odd about our manias. On a practical level, they may quickly gain popularity, but it takes us a long time to understand them. The driving mania, for example, became much more than just the sum of cars plus roads—it became a way of life, of structuring business, trade, and society. And eventually even a way of thinking. As a child of the 1940s, I grew up along with the automobile in Sweden. When my father bought a car in 1947, it was a big event both for him and for the whole town. He wanted to take us kids for a test drive in the car. But from the nearby paper mill I had just taken some little pieces of cardboard to put in the spokes of my bicycle, and they clattered magnificently as I rode. Since then, I've heard over and over how I didn't want to go along on the first car ride, preferring instead to clatter around on my bike.

I guess I've always been that kind of person: someone who's a bit different, although I too live in the age of the driving mania. I own a car, but I don't like to use it very often. I'd rather ride my bicycle, preferably at what I call "bike germination speed," which is perfect for allowing me to absorb sights, sounds, and smells. Of course, the driving mania also has a vise grip on me and my thoughts. Driving is a prerequisite for so much that goes on around me, and it has a decisive impact on my everyday life.

Right now the computer mania has moved to the forefront. The very fact that we're living in a time when information technology first appeared in our language is exciting. In the summer of 1994, IT was quite an exotic term in Swedish newspapers, but by the summer of 1995 it was hard to find a newspaper that didn't mention IT at least once. And since the summer of 1996, IT is used everywhere.

But doesn't the phrase Thoughts Take Time also apply to computers? Yes and no. In practical terms, information technology has simply poured out. You might say, "Information takes no time" (ITNT). Thoughts can't really keep up, and new ways of thinking will have to wait. If ITNT represents the *Information Convenience Store*, then TTT represents the *Temple of Ideas*.

The computer mania is going to be something quite different than the sum of modems, computers, E-mail addresses, and so on, just as the driving mania became something more than the sum of cars and roads. If you try to speculate about what the computer mania might become, it's good to keep in mind that historical experience has shown us that "more" doesn't necessarily mean more. It often simply means *different.*

Faster isn't just faster. Faster is also different. And the change will happen much more quickly with the computer mania than with the driving mania. The time ratio might even be 1 to 10. In the case of the driving mania, the upheaval of ideas and their incorporation into human activity took fifty years; the information technology up-heaval may take only five.

The Tele-perspective and the Environment

A very large part of the current environmental problem is actually a side effect of contemporary human culture assuming that there isn't enough time. Not enough of what I've described in this book as the only capital we possess. In the future, human beings will be either good or bad natural resources, depending on how they administer their relationship to time.

We think that we've removed most barriers of

distance. We think that we can administer global interaction based on "tele."

Compensating for our biological limits, we've become very good at tele. Human beings can't hear across great distances. That's why they invented the telephone—tele-sound. They can't see very far either. That's why they invented television, that is, the technique that makes it possible to see things from far away. In addition to the telephone and television and other tele-information, today we practice tele-consumption and also spread a lot of tele-garbage (waste and emissions released into the air, ground, and water). But not everything is suited to this tele-perspective. For one thing, I doubt whether we are enriched by tele-knowledge. Knowledge and information are not at all the same thing. Can all human interaction really take place on a tele basis? Can you become tele-wise? Can you make tele-peace? Can you take tele-responsibility?

Rapid Tele-Upheavals and Slow National Conservatism

Small-scale idea systems can be considerably more difficult to change than those on a global scale. Just compare the speed in the upheaval of the world's economic system to the obstinacy with which people cling to the old measuring systems in England, Canada, and the United States. In spite of grandiose international statements, they refuse in practice to switch over to the metric system and measure length in meters and weight in kilograms. The old system is deeply ingrained: why should they change something (inches, feet, yards, miles) that's practically in their genes and switch to measuring things in unfamiliar meters? Although claiming to have an international outlook, the individual remains remarkably conservative and insular!

Fast Food vs. Slow Food

In many areas, fast food has beat out slow food. As a trade-off, we've eliminated the fragrance of newly baked bread, different taste experiences, and the indefinable pleasure of a busy kitchen. Above all, we've changed the daily rhythm. Slow food wasn't ready right away. You had to wait for it. You might start feeling hungry. Maybe it was even a little boring to wait. Waiting is not a bad countermeasure to haste.

Globalization and Speed

From the world of the kitchen to the big world and its thought patterns. "I think we've been duped!"

said professor of ecology Torbjörn Fagerström early one summer evening in July 1997. That was the start of a long discussion. Not about simple solutions or about how things were better in the past. Instead, we began by asking ourselves: What kind of progress has been made, and how do we perceive it? Fagerström was a child of the industrial society, since he grew up in the 1950s. Back then there were schools and hospitals and in many ways it was a good life, but it didn't cost nearly as much as our present modern life does.

Have things really got better? And where has all the money gone? Could it be that the monetary system has been transformed into two systems that are only ostensibly linked? One fast and one slow? And without our noticing it—simply because Thoughts Take Time.

There was once a time when we used money as the means of exchange for goods and services. You could go to work, collect your wages, and then pay for your rent and food. But starting ten years ago, the security and independence of this method of exchange were undermined by the second economic system, the global network. In this system, electronic money is traded for electronic money without the intermediate stage of goods and services. You don't even have to carry out an electronic transaction: expectations are sufficient. Soon the old goods-services-money system will be scuttled forever.

Some might claim that there's a Swedish crisis or an Asian one, that the unrest has to do with a collapse of confidence in one country or in one part of the world. But that's a way of thinking that belongs to the old days, when money had real value. That relation disappeared when the wheels began to turn without the stability created by the friction against the real world. It's friction that makes ignition, acceleration, steering, and stopping possible.

The old economic system of goods, services, and money had a built-in inertia. You can't produce goods at any speed you like. You can't hire people at any speed you like either. You can't even fire them at any speed you like. This was what gave the old system its inertia, while the new system has no inertia whatsoever. Money is exchanged for money in fractions of a second.

Maybe we need to supplement the United Nations Security Council with a Council for Economic Security. Rather than the EU, European Union, what we need is a GU, Global Union. The impact of how we live has become global, and the administration should be appropriately placed, at

the level where the impact is felt. At the same
time, everyone realizes that we would never accept
a global ruler. It's even doubtful whether we would
accept a European ruler. (At least it seems to me
that there's occasionally a lot of rumbling between
the national leaders and the European ones.)

The changes in the world economy are genuinely new, as are the changes in environmental
development. What's happening is not a repetition of previous fluctuations in the world economy. For the first time, both economics and
ecology have become global in practice. In practice, but not in our world of ideas. Not yet.

Growing Chasms

The world is full of inequalities. The chasms are
unfathomably great. But even worse—and this is
where the time perspective comes in—the chasms
are growing. They're growing so fast that the acceleration makes it almost impossible to understand what's happening. This kind of acceleration
counteracts the trends toward solidarity that exist
within and between nations, between rich and
poor, and between different cultures. No one can
really manage to orient himself in this new world,
not even on a personal level. When so many negative things are going on, it's very easy to place

the blame for evil elsewhere. Always someplace else, never here. The result is a growing animosity toward anything foreign. So here we are in the midst of our tele-world, with a growing sense of alienation. Thoughts take such a long time!

The generation gap has also been affected. If the rate of change multiplies in a few years, the difference between people born in 1995 and in 2000 will be just as great as the difference once was between two generations. What will this mean for various professions? Will the teachers age much faster in relation to their students than they did in the past?

TTT—Could There Be More Good than Bad in It?

If I put together all the section heads of this chapter, I see a rather gloomy list:

- the need to be needed
- all these manias
- the tele-perspective and the environment
- rapid tele-upheavals and slow national conservatism
- fast food vs. slow food
- globalization and speed
- growing chasms

Of course it's unfortunate we're so slow that we can't manage to expose and prevent rapidly enough the bad things that are done in the name of progress. And yet how lucky we are that our thoughts don't coincide with the rate of progress. It may turn out that this very slowness is our best collective life insurance.

Chapter Six

Being in the Here and Now

The feeling of being at once in the here and now can be very strong. A few years ago at an art exhibit I saw an etching by Helena Plato. The image wasn't particularly remarkable, just a few pillars. The phrase "being here" suddenly occurred to me. Then I went over and looked at the title: "Being Now." Ever since I've had that etching hanging right inside the front door of my house. Here I am, I think every time I see it. Here I am. Now!

Being in the here and now isn't always combined in exactly that way. Sometimes being here may mean returning to a specific place that you once knew well and then discovering long-term changes. "This mountain ash tree has been here for fifty years. Now it looks as if the lichen is about

to smother it. And it happened so fast." Sometimes your presence may be felt by someone even
though the two of you are far from each other.
Sometimes you may feel yourself in the here and
now, no matter where you physically find yourself. The title of this chapter is worth thinking
about; it's much more than a cliché.

With a cell phone it's easy to break the bond
between here and now. "You always have 'here'
with you" was the refrain on a popular Swedish
TV program. And in some sense that's true. Can
you also say that you always have "now" with
you? Maybe. In the best-case scenario, you can at
least have your own now with you.

What makes me prefer both snail mail and
E-mail over phone conversations is that I get to
have my own now relatively undisturbed. This is
a freedom you can grant yourself these days, independent of time. That's not the way things were
when a person's actions had a direct effect on what
another person might do at the same time or a
second later. Back then people in conversation
shared the present moment.

Even space was fixed. A few generations ago,
an individual had no particular effect on anything
that was more than a couple of kilometers away.
Nor did anything far away affect the individual to

any appreciable degree. If a man mismanaged his land, he alone was responsible for his actions. Today every Swede travels an average of fifty kilometers a day. All kinds of transportation make distant places seem much closer. So can we now talk about a global here and now? Are human beings prepared to take on a global worldview? I don't think so.

It's possible that the arctic tern has a global worldview. It flies back and forth between the Arctic and Antarctic so many times in its life that the distance it covers corresponds to the distance between the earth and the moon. Presumably the bird must have a global worldview to manage something like this. A human being, on the other hand, wasn't meant to travel between the poles; as a matter of fact, we become disoriented when we move only a hundred kilometers or so. Without the help of technology, we were made to stay within a restricted geographical area. With technology our territory gets larger—but it's not unlimited.

Original Home

"Of course you know that I'm your mother's mother, don't you? And that she lived here with me when she was little?"

"I guess so, but where was *I* then?"

"Well, you weren't born yet. Back then the dollhouse belonged to her."

"But where *was* I?"

"When she was as little as Beatrice is now, she couldn't have been your mother, could she? You weren't born yet!"

"Yes, but where *was* I?"

I like the three-year-old's stubbornness. He can accept that there was a time when he wasn't yet born. But if that was true, then where *was* he? His concept of time and space is so definite, clear, and logical. Until he asked the question, it hadn't even occurred to me. And yet I've speculated a great deal about the same question from another perspective: how unborn children influence our actions today. I don't mean those who already exist in the womb and will soon be born. Or our future great-, great-, great-, great-, great-grandchildren. I mean unknown unborn children, in the distant future. Their future existence affects our actions every single day. But I never managed to think the same way going backward. To do that, I needed the help of a little child.

Maybe the thought "I must have existed somewhere before I was born" is behind the interest so many people have today in genealogy. There's a desire to link the past to some spatial home.

The Concept of "Here"

As I see it, a human being is not free of time or space. He is to a high degree a local phenomenon. Everything he does happens in a specific place at a specific time. In this sense his network must also be dependent on time and space. One summer day when I was picking currants, I started wondering in what contexts I would feel comfortable using that little word "here." I realized that I could quite easily say "here among the berry bushes." I could also say "here in Österlen" (which is where the berry bushes were located). I could say "here in Lund," "here in Skåne," "here in Sweden." But I couldn't imagine myself saying "here in Europe."

This really doesn't have anything to do with Sweden's being a new member of the EU. Of course we've abolished travel and passport restrictions within Europe, we have a free exchange of goods and services, common norms, and a language that we're gradually agreeing on. Soon we may have the same money and maybe even the same foreign policy and defense. But none of this is enough to make me able to say "here in Europe."

I think quite frankly that my European network of people is too sparse for that. My contacts are too few and above all too sporadic. Let's think a little more about networks—a concept that I think is central to the here and now.

The Now in Networks

Everybody has his own network. The very young child encounters a small community in his personal childhood: there are only a few people around him. What affects the child's personality the most is how these people live on a daily basis, how they treat each other, how they deal with and solve problems.

After a few years, he encounters his cultural childhood at the day-care center, at school, on the playground, and so on. The network grows bigger and the personal space gets relatively smaller. The most important requirement for the adults surrounding the child is that they be able to connect with the child's personal childhood. Otherwise everything becomes irrelevant. The worst thing is for the child to feel so alienated, so anonymous, that he experiences other people as replaceable. Or even feels that he himself is replaceable. Day-care teachers may come and go—but the gallery of people surrounding a child cannot keep perpetually changing. There must be at least some adults who are always there. A here-and-now presence is required of other people.

Without these fixed points to hold on to, the child may lose his grip and later contribute to creating a society filled with violence. If a person has a firmly established sense that his fellow human beings are replaceable, it won't make much difference if he shoots someone. The individual no longer has a face. On the other hand, if you recognize both yourself and your fellow human beings as unique individuals, it's clear that no law of interchangeability will apply. Instead, a personal identity emerges within a personal space, in a personal time, and with the potential for creating a personal network with other people.

Imprinting and Self-Image

A human being undergoes imprinting all his life, but he experiences the strongest imprinting during childhood. My childhood network was quite sparse because I was born out in the country. My network included only a few people, but they stayed with me for a long time. These were the people who gave me my self-image. Their reactions, expressed through words, body language, and behavior, and the human interaction between them and me were crucial to my development. It's probably that way for all children. Human interaction is culture—and this is probably what our "here" is. Community is the core of culture. A lack of culture means to reject, to abandon.

Being Here in Crowds, Being Here in Solitude

"Solitude, Bodil, solitude is a person's worst enemy," my uncle Erik once told me. He was standing in the courtyard of Hult Farm in Småland. It was getting on toward fall. As he spoke, I thought I could hear the approach of winter, snow, and isolation. Even though I'm a semihermit myself, even though I gladly seek out solitude, I think I understood what Uncle Erik meant. If a person doesn't have a network within reach, his self-image will crumble.

Of course it's easier for people on the periphery than in the middle of the city. The global trend is for the city center to become, relatively speaking, more and more high-density. In Sweden, 83% of the population now lives in cities. Nine out of ten children grow up in cities. It's hard to believe that most of us, especially in the summer, still have such a longing for nature. As of the year 2000, more than half the world's population lives in cities. At the turn of the previous century, it was only 12%. And the cities are just getting bigger and bigger. Today only Tokyo has more than 20 million inhabitants, but by 2015 there may be seven cities with a population greater than 20 million.

From 12% of the world's population to 50%—and in only one century. What is this "Urban" causing urbanization? Could it be a combination of three of humanity's strongest driving forces: laziness, material comfort, and the urge for greater individual freedom of action? Is that the kind of "being here" that we're looking for in the multiplicity of the cities? Or is it the pulse that draws us? We want to have everything *all at once*! Maybe it's the urgent pace that we seek rather than the density of living.

I don't have the answers. But I do know that the driving forces are one thing, the effects quite another. Was it better with the rather monotonous and permanent network of the village? Was the key to a person's self-image any more accessible there? It's not easy to predict what will work for one person and what will work for another. That's exactly why the movement from the country to the city is intense, to say the least. Within a few generations in Sweden we have fundamentally changed the conditions for raising our children, conditions that affect their self-image and their perception of time.

Being Here Via Overlapping Networks

If you're Swedish and go down the list of several hundred people you know or know of, there's a big chance that I'll know at least a few of them. Our Swedish networks overlap. It's this overlapping of networks that makes it possible for us to say that we belong together, to the same culture and the same society.

Without the overlapping of networks, a society would collapse like a house of cards. One clear example from our day and age is the swift fall of the Eastern European nations. People in those countries had constricted their networks because they could never be sure whom they could trust or who was an informer. The travel ban also played a role in reducing individual networks. The overlapping of networks became so slight that there was no built-in stability to offset things when the power base of society began to falter. A house of cards collapses when the wind blows.

We now have networks and overlappings on the Internet that were never before anticipated. It's a tremendously huge net, and yet it's not too big, because each user builds his own net the way he wants it. You can see as far as you want to see, and the personal Internet horizon is eminently mobile. You overlap only with those you choose to overlap with.

Being Now in Your Own Thoughts

No one, not even a scientist, has the answers to all the new questions that keep popping up. But the awareness that people can think for themselves means that we don't need to feel too uneasy about all the unanswered questions. The best strategy is to encourage the ability to think for yourself, and to communicate with others. The worst of all strategies would be to contribute to creating a society of citizens who, bewildered and unthinking, sit down and wait for a strong leader to solve their problems. There is always someone who claims to have the answers. It's when "everybody" believes in and follows this type of leader that something, such as an environmental accident, can become truly dangerous.

The alternative is a swarm of people, businesses, and networks. Somewhere within this swarm can be found a dynamic stability, a place where you can find repose while being in the midst of activity. If we think the changes are happening too fast now, I'm sure it's nothing compared to what it'll be like in the future. That's why we have to be able to rest by being in the now in our own thoughts.

Today, many people are saying that they feel worn out by all the rapid changes. With development that takes place even faster, we won't be able to make sporadic giant leaps, only later to say; "No, by God, I've made enough changes, so things will just have to stay the way they are for a few years. I'm not going to make any more changes for a long time." Giant leaps followed by stagnation are in reality nothing more than a lurching movement. If the lurching increases, it becomes continuous movement. Then we have to find rest in movement rather than in tranquillity.

Does Spacelessness Exist?

Existential questions about life and death are in essence timeless. But what we sometimes call a "timeless style" is not really timeless. It might last a few decades, but I can guarantee that it won't last a century.

What about spacelessness—does it exist? Over the past fifty years, in quite a remarkable way, we have virtually abolished distance. We count hours rather than kilometers now. The distance between two places is no longer very important. What's important is how quickly we can get from one place to another. Geographically, the old "here" and "there" have lost their significance. And yet human beings are supremely local. The question is whether we are capable of conceiving of anything other than length, area, and volume, that is, something that resembles our own height and reach.

We often think in terms of spacelessness. In our thoughts we stop calculating distance: We think we understand nature and the environment without connecting them to their space, their locality. Of course, we don't talk about the spacelessness of our thoughts. Because then we'd hear how foolish it sounds to disregard local and regional peculiarities. It's easy enough, for example, to see that sometimes those who plan the construction of tunnels and bridges don't respect the insights and experience of the local populace.

How Can You Create a Sense of the Here and Now?

In his memoirs, Bertrand Russell described what made life worth living for him:

- the search for knowledge
- a longing for love
- an empathy with those who are suffering

He wrote this from a personal, individual perspective. I think that it's when you're able to live according to these three values that you're in the here and now. If you're not able to live this out in reality—and if you have the gift of imagination—then you can retreat into your inner space. This retreating is rarely valued by the rest of the world. How many kids have been told, "Don't just sit there daydreaming!" Actually, such a talent might be the very best thing, and should not be suppressed. It can help a child later in life to achieve what is outwardly important: the search for knowledge, a longing for love, and an empathy with those who are suffering. But this outward attitude has to come when the child is ready and able to embrace it. The inner dream life may be helpful and necessary for a while.

Is it possible to create a collective sense of being in the here and now side by side with mass rallies, rock concerts, and sports arenas? I thought about this when I attended the Globe 1998 Conference and listened to an Indonesian named Gede Raka. He was talking about how to make a creative environment, and suddenly he was saying words that were familiar to me. He said that the mark of a creative environment is whether it

- is conducive to learning
- intends to do good things
- is conducive to friendships

No one can ignore the obvious similarities between the insights of Bertrand Russell and Gede Raka, although they apparently arose independently of each other.

If I had to use only one sentence to illustrate being in the here and now, it would be this: Being in the here and now makes for a creative environment.

Chapter Seven

The Pace of Change and the Perception of Time

So far in this book I've argued that human beings are not particularly good at *measuring* clock time inside their own bodies. I've talked about how the other type of time, a person's experienced time, is influenced not only by absolute minutes but also by the quality of time: the lack of interruptions, the setup time, and so on. But just like plants, fruit flies, and bacteria, we also have built-in clocks. Before we constructed external clocks, we were completely dependent on our inner clocks. Now we have two clock functions, the outer and the inner, and we've discovered our ability to adapt in terms of time. This is an ability that is both one of our biggest strengths and one of our biggest weaknesses.

When we come up with a technology that

requires a pace entirely different from that in the past, we adapt to the new conditions—in spite of the fact that we're not biologically equipped for them. For example, people are able to change time zones. After a few days of jet lag, the body adjusts. We can adapt to sitting in a car traveling 110 km/ hour and think we're capable of mastering the situation and experiencing our surroundings as if they're standing still. We don't take into account the "pace lag," because a human being can adapt his perception of time to the pace with which his surroundings change.

That's what I'll talk about in this chapter.

Most often it's technological changes that have created the conditions for other changes, which in turn have affected you. So many things are interconnected. It's no coincidence, for example, that apartheid in South Africa collapsed at about the same time as the wall fell between East and West. When absurdities continue despite the fact that the arenas are now open, they dig their own graves. In the early 1990s the American TV station CNN broadcast directly from the site of the leadership coup in Russia, which was attempting to overthrow *glasnost.* What would have happened if this openness via technology hadn't existed there? Would the outcome of the coup have been different?

It's no coincidence that the world economy is now a global one. It's the global digital networks that provide the technological basis on which everything rests. And it's no coincidence that right now students are more interested in searching than in receiving. Today they have the strong support of technology to help them search.

Pace Lag

When I think about the occasion of the first moon landing in 1969, it seems almost unimaginably distant. If I think about it some more, I realize that by that time I had been alive for twenty-seven years, almost half my present age. If I think ahead, I know that neither I nor anyone else has any idea what will happen in the future. But there's one thing I know for sure: the changes during the next twenty-seven years will be even greater than what they were during my first twenty-seven years.

How can civilization cope with this? Everything is going faster, faster, faster. People are starting to react. They resist. Their bodies rebel. I think there's only one way to counteract it: by trying to find some sort of repose in movement itself.

Here we can turn to the ancient Greeks and their teachings. We will find nothing about movement itself, because they believed that what moves, what is changeable, cannot be studied. Whenever you try to go back to it, it's no longer there. But there are still certain parts of their teachings that have inspired me and that I will try to apply to the context of change.

Plato said that a horse in the pasture is not as important as the idea behind all horses, the very essence of being a horse. This essence is eternal, while the living horses are merely imperfect manifestations of the idea. Just imagine if we started thinking about technology in this way. Then we'd look for the essence of technology, the idea itself behind all these imperfect manifestations, all these gadgets and other things with which we surround ourselves.

Clock Essence, the Idea of the Clock

Take, for example, the clock. What purpose does it serve? Once upon a time the clock was created to be something resembling the universe (the sundial, the cathedral clock, even the ordinary pocket watch with hands). Clock time was a serene and splendid representation of the sun's passage across the sky—as perceived by human beings. Then more and more refined ways of measuring time came about, culminating in the digital clock. One of its distinguishing features is that it tells us nothing whatsoever about the universe.

Could the digital clock be a symptom of the fact that we've achieved a precision that may be relevant for both the micro- and macrocosm but tells us nothing about the universe? Could it be a symptom of a breach of concept that is actually more profound than we initially thought? Could it be that the very concept of the clock, the clock essence, is no longer to show the natural course of time but, rather, artificial time, time as an artifact?

Industrialization and the Clock

Why do we chase after time the way we do? One important reason is that we've adapted ourselves to the thought patterns of the industrial era. Industrialization meant that we fell completely into the clutches of artificial time. As I mentioned earlier, the rise and subsequent fall of industrialization have also distorted our perception of what work is and how we value it.

Let me start a hundred years ago. In 1899, people fought an intense battle against working themselves to death. No one in 1899 would have been able to comprehend something as absurd as trying to create work. They strove to be free from work or to be unemployed. Someone in 1899 would never have uttered the word "unemployment" with sorrow in his voice. Instead, he would have asked with amusement, "Do you mean to tell me you actually did it? That you won't have to work yourself to death?"

But both back then and today there exists one fundamental prerequisite: a person wants to feel needed. Sometimes I think we should institute an Unemployment Department with an Unemployment Minister. This minister would not combat unemployment. Instead he or she would safeguard it and see to it that so-called unemployed people are needed and feel needed. Because there's an endless number of things to be done, but there's nothing that says they have to be done using the old work patterns.

Conditioning

Today we're left with a relic of industrialization: the clock and its dominance. Our training in this area has substantial overtones of conditioning. We react reflexively to the clock and its regulation of all our time. We react just as strongly to the idea that there is work that needs to be done.

The golden age of industrialization is over, and it's possible that very soon just as few people will be employed in industry as in agriculture today. The thought patterns of industrialization have become outmoded. But they still prevail and hold our thoughts captive, partially by means of the clock. Industrialization has conquered other parts of our lives as well. Just think about all those nice terms like *efficiency, automation, work hours,* and *time off.* Trouble arises if you unsuspectingly try to apply them to work based on human inter-action, such as social services or education, or to intellectual work, such as research or learning. It will be even more ridiculous if the thought pat-terns of industrialization are allowed to permeate businesses in the future. Surely we know that human interaction can't be automated or regu-lated. Surely we know that intellectual work, such as research (the creation of new knowledge) and learning (the creation of new knowledge within oneself), must be measured in a way totally dif-ferent from the way we measure the work of in-dustrialization. "Of course we know that," I say. Not so. I should ask instead, "When will we 'know'? When will we have good alternatives?" It's going to take a long time if we don't start unlearning old ways now. What we need is think-ology rather than technology.

Thinkology vs. Technology

The prerequisites for future thinkology have been seriously reduced by the fact that industrialization has been followed by the information and media society. Talk about an accelerated rate of change! One of the dilemmas of our era is the nonstop nature of the media and the fear of deviating from a bland facade, for example on TV. We rarely get to participate in anything that might be slightly difficult; rarely is there anything that involves us. Everyone is so afraid that the TV viewers will zap over to another channel. Adaptation becomes a destructive cycle. The easier the contents are to digest, the less patience the public will have—and the more zap-happy they'll be. The expectations become self-fulfilling.

I wonder whether it might be time for a different channel in our digital TV era. I think there's commercial potential for a channel with the working title "Enticements for the TV-Distressed." It would be directed at those of us who have stopped watching TV, not only because we're unhappy with the content but also because watching TV has made us nervous. "Enticements for the TV-Distressed" would proudly promise, "Here you won't be subjected to commercials. If we do have commercials, they'll be at least an hour long. And you won't be subjected to amateurishly produced short trailers that break in and destroy the mood."

With that kind of channel we would feel secure in the knowledge that now and then our minds could take sufficiently long breaks. We could avoid extreme upheavals that merely lead to indifference. A channel made for us, the "non-zapping generation," who give priority to content that is thoughtful and high-quality, with gentle, continuous segues between programs.

Thought Inertia

As long as the rate of development was moderate, our ability to recognize old thought patterns was a good way to preserve contact with our cultural heritage and to pass it on. "Everything is as it always has been and as it always will be." But when the rate of change becomes too great, when our patterns of interpretation become increasingly outmoded, it may be better to question the old ways of thinking rather than try to interpret each new situation with old eyes. This won't be easy.

One obstacle is not only the conservative nature of our thoughts but also the resistance of our bodies. Evolution has a pronounced "pace lag."

Take our eyesight, for instance. Our vision is good straight ahead, but peripherally it's so poor that we catch only glimpses of what we're passing. No doubt this was sufficient as long as we moved at speeds that we could manage under our own power. Our eyesight was not especially suited to galloping on horseback, but with our peripheral vision we managed relatively well. A warning from the side prompted the individual to turn his head sharply, and he was then able to distinguish any possibly dangerous impediments or objects.

In the age of the automobile, things are quite different. Our peripheral vision isn't good enough to warn us in time of a child rushing out into the street or an approaching moose. It may be possible to develop aids for our peripheral vision (work is under way), but that doesn't change the basic fact: a human being's eyesight isn't designed for high-speed movement.

The Lack of Speed Phobias

It's worth considering that development may have occurred so fast that human beings haven't managed to develop any speed phobias. In other areas evolution has had enough time so that a number of dangerous situations give us phobias. This includes heights, open spaces, closed rooms, spiders, and snakes. But since the capabilities for rapid transportation are still relatively new, no proper warning systems have yet been developed.

What can we do in the absence of a "too-fast" reflex? There's actually a lot we can do. To start with, we can draw on parts of old thought patterns: the collective common sense. This has been developed over many, many generations. One example of the collective common sense still prevalent when I was growing up was that everyone knew, without any kind of research, that you don't feed dead animals to vegetarians (cows).

Common Sense

Even the collective common sense needs to be examined with a good dose of skepticism. It can't be so simple that you can just hide behind it. The collective common sense, with its ancient insights, has a greater chance of lasting in the long term than something based on outmoded ideas. Many of the thought patterns that have developed over the past fifty years may in the long run turn out to be mere fads. In your mind try to mark all thought patterns from the year 1950 with the label "Best if used before 1-1-1999." This sort of labeling should force us to look for alternatives, or for good reasons to extend the expiration date.

Just imagine if this skepticism could teach us to watch out for every group of people consisting of individuals that are the same age or the same sex. In this day and age we should regard groups that are uniformly one age or one sex as warning signs. We have sufficient evidence now that demonstrates what happens when human beings, by restricting themselves to an "elite," institute changes that turn out to be completely wrong ten or twenty years later. Mad cow disease, for instance. What can we learn for the future from this contravention of good sense, one of the most perverse of our time? What prompted the idea to feed cadavers to grass-grazing animals that would later become food for humans? Just for a moment forget about science and speculations about what happens on the cellular level in the cows. Instead think about how this strange decision was made by human beings: small groups of people, cells of people. I think that decisions such as feeding vegetarians with cannibal food can be made only in small or overly homogeneous circles. In groups where one person slaps another on the back and says, "Fine, fine, my dear fellow, of course that's what we're going to do," and then receives a slap on the back in return.

It's in small human cells like this that people can lose contact with the collective common sense, which has been passed down through the whole history of civilization. To keep it alive we need mixed groups of old and young, men and women, scientists and laypersons.

The Pace Lag of Research

Even in research, the so-called leading edge of humanity toward the future, speed can threaten the very core of the activity. How are we going to study what's new? Who is going to study what's new? And who is going to designate and study those who do the studies? If you try to safeguard quality but have only the criteria and concepts of current research to go on, there's a big danger that you will never make innovations. It may be justified to fear that the obstacles to genuinely new scientific advances may be too great.

By what right will newcomers be able to argue against what is established and (measured by its own standards) of high quality? The new do not have the old qualifications to rely on, and perhaps no clear methods to refer to. This mix of potential genius and potential charlatanism is impossible to penetrate. We don't know how to study what's new, since such advances may be unusable as a basis for decisions in the existing system.

I'll bet one thing though: it isn't going to get any easier. In fact, it will get harder as the growth of knowledge increases at a faster and faster rate. More scientists are at work today than the sum of all scientists who previously existed. And one society after another is striving to become more knowledge-based. In other words, we're in the midst of an extraordinary exponential growth in research.

Exponential Functions

What is an exponential function? You've probably seen lots of curves that either rise sharply after a slow start or fall quickly and then level off. Moving either toward heaven or toward hell. They all have the same fundamental background.

Let me try to explain this background. If you start feeling nauseated after a few lines, just skip to the next section. But if you follow the reasoning about the pond and the water lilies below, you'll learn something that may prove useful to you in many contexts. Besides, it's impossible for me to finish writing a book on 1-1-1999 with the title *Unwinding the Clock* without getting to the bottom of exponential functions. But I promise: no mathematical formulas.

In a pond with water lilies, the number of water lilies doubles each year. Originally there are only a few patches, maybe one-thirty-second of the pond's surface is covered by water lilies. Everyone thinks the pond is lovely, including those who swim in it. The same holds true for the following year, when the water lilies cover one-sixteenth of the surface. But then things start to speed up. The next year one-eighth of the pond is covered with water lilies, a year later one-fourth, and the year after that half the pond. Starting with the year that half the surface is covered with water lilies, there is a maximum of one year left before the entire surface will consist of water lilies.

Take a piece of paper and pen and sketch this out. Do you see how treacherous the development is? On the one hand, the rate doesn't change—none of the water lilies is the source of either more or fewer water lilies in year five than in year one. But since more and more water lilies are appearing, there are more that can reproduce. And more and more. This distinguishes all exponential functions: the individual growth is constant, but the total increases faster and faster.

There are also declining exponential functions, circumstances in which something diminishes in scope at every moment at a constant rate of decrease per existing unit. The decrease is very sharp at the beginning and then later flattens out, as there are fewer and fewer left which can diminish in scope. Radioactive decay is a classic example of a declining exponential function. After one half-life, half the number of the original radioactive atoms remain. After another half-life, one-fourth remain; after three half-lives, one-eighth; and so on.

Exponential functions are found in many biological and physical contexts, such as the growth of bacteria or the increase or decrease in population of rabbits within a specific area. In practice, increasing biological exponential functions are broken after awhile when another biological phenomenon (or medicine, pesticide, or the like) takes over.

On the other hand, technology's exponential functions (for instance, the spread of information technology) are not held in check by any other exponential functions. For that reason, they can go a long way, even though you and I are not particularly exponential in our temperament. On the contrary—we're largely creatures of habit. If we are nevertheless subjected to exponential functions that have a strong impact on us, our perception of time can be fundamentally changed. Either we feel as if time is simply running away from us or we feel as if so much has changed that it couldn't possibly have happened in just one year—it must have taken two or three or ten years!

It's more common for us to be struck by the feeling that time is running away from us than by the feeling that the year has become longer. But recently I've also experienced the latter. Maybe even right now, as I'm writing this.

The information society, the Internet, and everything that's happening inside me are all so revolutionary that all my previous experience tells me it's unlikely that these new things could have occurred in such a short time. It's the same kind of feeling you might have when you come back from vacation—it feels as if you've been gone for a very long time. When there are great upheavals, we lose our grip on the time scale.

The Runaway Development of Knowledge

You may harbor a justifiable fear that the runaway development of knowledge contains negative elements. Let's assume that we decided in advance that all new knowledge was bad. What would that kind of outlook be able to prevent? I don't know. I really don't know. Many people, including myself, are basically inquisitive. Can't help wondering. Can't ignore that one answer leads to the next question.

What would be the countermeasure to prevent the exponential functions of knowledge from destroying all humanity? You should know that while "many merely sit and stare, up at the TV or down at their chair," a great deal is happening in research that will turn ancient concepts upside down. To date, Dolly the cloned sheep is probably the most spectacular example. But this is just the beginning. Consider the following statements:

- Human beings are on their way to describing, reshaping, and creating life.
- Human beings are on their way to uncovering the ancient relationship between sexuality and reproduction.
- Human beings are on their way to making the boundary between life and death less distinct.
- Human beings are on their way, via computer technology, to uncovering some of the mysteries of learning.

Run through these statements several times in your mind or say them out loud. "On their way" indicates an ongoing process, and in the future the breakthroughs will start pouring in. Over the course of only a few years, fundamental human ideas may be changed in a way that will affect everyone's daily life.

What kind of security is there in such a world? Well, at least it's not the old, ordinary kind of security. We can't rely on society, formal organizations, or even competing exponential functions in the world of ideas to keep each other in check the way they do in the material world. The only model I think we can bring along from the old world into the intangible one is expressed by Astrid Lindgren in her book *Pippi Longstocking.* Loosely quoted: "Whoever is very strong has to be very kind."

Goodwill, Expertise, and the Courage of Your Convictions

In terms of kindness, I think we scientists are pretty much like people in general; kindness is not necessarily a given. People are changed through interaction with their environment; scientists are too. Let's assume that everyone, or almost everyone, became more oriented toward seeking knowledge. Assume that more people fully understood how challenging the consequences of the exponential growth of knowledge are. Assume that many people focused on research about human beings and their striving for knowledge.

One assumption after another—what would this lead to? A small elite, don't you think? The star scientists do comprise an extremely small elite, it's true. But theories and methods also exist outside science. Just look at the little child who each day masters new associations, meaning new theories. They don't have to be true; they may not even last until the next day. But as long as an individual has use for his own theories, as long as his thoughts are marked by a certain economy (they allow him to think economically) and don't disturb the people around him, I would recommend a generosity of ideas. Both to protect the security a person inherently feels when he can think for himself (see below) and because it will be much more pleasant this way.

It's only when someone wants to demonstrate that he's "right" that he has to be able to prove the elegance of his theory. Otherwise no one will accept a change in the old ways of thought that have required blood, sweat, and tears to establish.

It would be best if we could keep alive Kant's definition of enlightenment:

- Enlightenment is man's liberation from his self-imposed immaturity.
- Immaturity is man's inability to think without the guidance of someone else.
- This immaturity is self-imposed when the cause is not a lack of understanding but rather a lack of decisiveness and courage.

A little comment on this point about courage. Several years ago there was an editorial in a Swedish newspaper. I can't remember what the subject was, but there was a blank graph with one axis for "goodwill" and another for "expertise." This is a good graph to keep in the back of your mind. Many times it has helped me in situations that otherwise would have just given me a rush of adrenaline. The combination "goodwill without expertise" is not good. Neither is the combination "expertise without goodwill." A moderate amount of goodwill combined with a comfortable amount of expertise is usually sufficient for a good result.

But sometimes a third quality is needed: the courage to stand up for your beliefs. For instance, in terms of the environmental stresses that human beings are now facing, it's not a lack of understanding that creates the greatest problems. Rather, it's precisely what Kant calls "lack of decisiveness and courage." That's why the graph for the development of ideas requires three axes: one for expertise, one for goodwill, and one for the courage of your convictions.

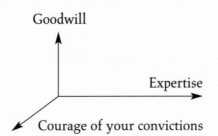

A diagram for you to use when thinking about rates of change and attitudes toward time. Go ahead and use it for your own examples!

Chapter Eight

Rhythm and Nonrhythm

Time is mirrored not only in clock time, in intervals of time, and in speeds but also in rhythms. And there are many kinds of rhythm: biological, social, intellectual, musical, and so on.

The physical concept that is associated with rhythm is frequency, which means how often something is repeated during a specific interval of time. If something occurs once per second, the frequency is 1 Hz (hertz). Your heart beats at a rate of about 1 Hz. If you exert yourself so that it beats faster, it can reach 2 or 3 Hz.

The rhythm of something occurring once per hour, meaning once per 3,600 seconds, is 1/3600 Hz or 0.3 mHz (millihertz). It goes without saying that if you try to combine something having a rhythm of 1 Hz with something else having a rhythm of mHz or μHz (microhertz), there will be problems. The reason I'm interested in rhythm is that I think the differences in rhythm are a largely ignored source of difficulties both between individuals and between human beings and their environment.

Differences between Thought Rhythms and Conversational Rhythms

Social and intellectual rhythms are significantly different. Thinking in a thousand different directions in quick succession takes almost no time at all. On the other hand, if you want to (or are forced to) recount your thoughts, you could talk forever and you still wouldn't explain all the intermediate steps. If you ever meet someone who thinks with the same rhythm and in the same direction as you do, you may feel a visceral joy that your rhythms match. Almost as on the dance floor.

A person's rhythm can vary, of course, but this doesn't prevent her from being disposed toward a specific, basic (thought) rhythm. This rhythm may be one of the most important characteristics distinguishing her from other people. The interplay between individual rhythms can have a great impact on human interaction.

It's fascinating to meet people whose rhythms agree with your own. Arne Svensk, one of my day-to-day colleagues, once drew my attention to the way thought rhythms can either unite or separate people. If the rhythms match, your generosity in terms of putting up with each other can be almost unlimited. But if the rhythms don't match, even the most trivial things can irritate you.

I think this may be a sign that our inner thought generators are largely built on random generators and timers. Random generators that sample and can learn from the results—that can create knowledge and feelings from our experiences. And timers that keep everything together and moving forward—timers that are individual.

Let's say that this image, in all its crudeness, contains at least a kernel of truth. Then it's not so strange that it's a tremendously positive experience if you're lucky enough to meet another person who has the same rhythm. You can sense the way thought meets thought, how the timers quite simply latch on to each other and move together. What joy to experience this for a brief moment! But it's almost impossible to establish any real contact with someone who has a completely different rhythm from your own. The two time systems drive you apart at once.

It's fascinating to think that there are other people in the world who, in at least some areas, have approximately the same rhythm, the same frequency, as you. You probably won't meet many of them. It's not similarities in rhythm that bring people together, but rather culture, religion, and perhaps specific interests—not to mention external circumstances.

We end up in small cells where we probably shouldn't be, since the most important factor—rhythm—may divide us. It's worth pondering a bit whether a person can have one or more individual basic frequencies in his mental and emotional life, much as you have a basic frequency in your voice. And maybe our basic thought and feeling frequencies influence not only our own experiences but also our interaction with other people.

No doubt it wouldn't be good if we were able to create cells that consisted solely of people with the same rhythm. But the risk of this is so infinitesimally small that I don't even need to warn against it. Instead, I suggest that more people should equip themselves with internal scouts on the lookout for people who have the same rhythm as themselves. Because it's so much fun when you find someone with the same thought rhythm.

Individual Rhythm

Individual—in/dividual = cannot be divided. A human being is an undivided entity. Most communication inside ourselves is not accessible to anyone else. Most of it isn't even available to us. But some of our thoughts are conscious, and those are the ones we can control.

Sometimes the variation in my own thought rhythm makes me giggle. Often it's so fast, occasionally much too fast, that the rest of me can't keep up. But sometimes it's almost unbearably sluggish—which now and then can be great. I might wake up with only one thought in my head, and this thought then revolves practically unchanged, ever so slowly. If the thought is a nice one, it's a particularly pleasant condition. Sometimes I'm also a one-thought thinker when I'm out jogging. The whole time, my mind can be filled with a single thought, often quite an unimportant one. Talk about taking a break!

Sometimes I think that high-frequency and low-frequency thinking competes simultaneously. Some rhythms may merge and be amplified; others are filtered out and washed away. Or sometimes an oddball thought takes over and dominates. The kind of thought that sticks so that it not only dominates but even resets the entire thought machinery to its own rhythm.

I have two internal images of the way rhythms compete or cooperate with each other. The first has to do with the dominant sea swell that you cannot fight; you simply have to go along and adapt to it. The second has to do with how this kind of large wave is composed of many smaller waves. Some manage to oscillate in tempo and in phase right from the beginning, amplifying each other for the big final wave; others can't hold on to the rhythm and are sucked down into the backwash.

Trendsetter Number 1

I'm now going to present a few trendsetters. There are several basic frequencies to the way I think, which my new thoughts follow and adapt to. These trendsetters have both interpretive and rhythmic precursors. They sweep the new rhythms along with them as an amplification of the rhythm that is already in place.

Take for example my first experience with existential solitude. It was triumphant. I was in the first grade in a small-town school; this was in the late 1940s. One day I suddenly had a flash of insight: "Nobody can know what I'm thinking, nobody can know what I'm thinking, nobody can know what I'm thinking." I'm sure this went round and round in my head, although I can't really remember it. But I do remember how I pressed my lips tightly together. The realization that my thoughts were mine, mine alone, and that they couldn't slip out, still remains a tactile and joyful memory. It's so strong that I can't help pressing my lips tightly together right now, at the very thought of it.

It might seem a little ridiculous to be sitting here pressing my lips together as I recount this episode. But in one way it's a good reminder: no one can go through my internal images and ponder over my feelings about time and rhythm. Everyone has to go through his own internal images. Whether you get anything out of this book depends more on what's between the lines, how you fill in the gaps yourself, than on what I've written.

A book like this can affect only what already exists inside you. It's just a matter of giving it a chance to emerge. In the best-case scenario, what's written here will resonate with an internal string that is already vibrating a little. When the vibration is amplified so that the string vibrates harder, you may experience unexpected new thoughts. But they might have been there for a very long time.

Trendsetter Number 2

I can attribute to my school days another strong memory of the way in which individuality plays a role in our lives. When I was twelve or thirteen years old, I had a handicrafts teacher who said something that prompted me to think, "Can you really say that?!" Of course I should have asked her, but I didn't dare. The situation was the least advantageous imaginable from a pedagogical standpoint. A teacher says something incomprehensible, and the pupil regards her as so imposing that she doesn't dare question it. But it had a long-lasting effect, to put it mildly—I still haven't forgotten it.

She said: *It's so individually individual!*

And there I stood, wondering whether the teacher had said something wise or something that was utter nonsense. I still don't know. Well, yes, as a matter of fact, I do—long ago I decided that this statement contains one of life's greatest wisdoms. I've got a lot of use out of the adage "It's

so individually individual." It helps me understand how two people who have been in the exact
same situation can still perceive it completely differently. When each of them later recalls the
situation in question, the individual quality of
the recollection process itself has turned the re-
membered images into caricatures of the original
impressions. Because of this, there's hardly anything except possible photographs (or potential
independent witnesses) to confirm that the two
people have experienced the same event. They
didn't have the same rhythm—it was not the same
events that turned internal oscillations into major
vibrations.

Trendsetter Number 3

In my early youth I saw a three-act play by Brecht.
Act 1: we see a woman sitting in a concentration
camp, wondering who could have turned her in.
She decides that it must have been her neighbors.
Act 2: we're at the neighbors' house. They weren't
the ones who informed on the woman. But now,
when she's about to be released after only six
months, they wonder what the reason could be.
They decide that she must have agreed to become
an informer, and that's why she's being released.

Act 3: the woman comes home and encounters her neighbors. Both parties make every effort to seem accommodating and trustworthy to each other—but it doesn't work!

Once a suspicion has taken root, it's extremely difficult to get rid of it. It's like two people on the dance floor who don't hear the same melody; rather, each person listens to his own. They neither can nor want to find a common rhythm.

A lack of interest can function in the same way as suspicion. Among my colleagues, for instance, there are individuals who have a keen intellect, great creativity, a solid capacity for work, and enormous integrity. But a few of them dislike mathematical symbols and structures. If I want to make a complicated argument a little easier (from my point of view) by adding a few figures or a table, I sometimes end up provoking outright opposition. The strings inside my audience that had just been vibrating in a strongly positive way abruptly come to a standstill.

Rhythms and Nonrhythms: Sevenfold

Of course we can adapt to rhythms, and of course we can tolerate nonrhythms—but only within limits. I conclude this chapter with a number of diverse examples, and maybe you can come up with examples of your own.

1. Outdoor rhythms

I belong to the majority of people who aren't particularly fond of ironing. But if I'm outdoors with the laundry, I forget all about the fact that ironing is boring. Sometimes I even enjoy ironing if I'm outside. You might think that I have this feeling because of the nice smells, the birds, and the gentle breeze. But there's something deeper stirring inside me—something that has to do with outdoor rhythms. There is a rhythm that suits me, a rhythm that is soothing to me. Indoors I turn to music, but no music can truly eradicate the tedium of ironing. By the way, my favorite ironing music is one of the Brandenburg concertos. You can go ahead and ask me why, but I won't be able to tell you.

2. Water rhythms

Many of us like to sit and just stare out at the sea. Or think. A creek, preferably with stones, also does nicely. By the sea it may be a matter of a feeling of infinity that is called forth in us—yes, a feeling of infinity is also a kind of rhythm, a rhythm with a zero frequency. There are many other rhythmic feelings that gently moving water can summon up, whether it's an ocean or a creek. Not to mention the flashing glints of the sun on a springtime stream!

3. A poor talent for rhythm

The capacity of a human being to adapt to rhythms may be fairly good, but it's nothing in comparison with that of a hummingbird. When a hummingbird sucks the nectar from a blossom that is swaying fiercely in the wind, the bird makes a movement that no human being could achieve. Our ability to adapt to rhythms is too poor.

4. Childhood rhythms and adult rhythms

Certain rhythms belong exclusively to childhood. The fact that children, for instance, have a rhythm that makes them hyperactive after a meal, whereas most grown-ups become drowsy after eating, is one of the many differences in rhythm between them.

5. Traffic rhythms

I don't know anyone who gets high from *listening* to traffic rhythms. But I'm sure such people do exist—it's so individually individual. But most people adapt themselves to the prevailing traffic rhythms. Those drivers who don't can often cause problems. Traffic rhythms are different at different times of the day. On the highway, the morning traffic is different from that of any other time. In the morning everyone maintains a steady and relatively high speed. No irritation, no tailgating, no wild swerving. Everyone sitting in that long, long line has sat there many, many times before. They've learned their morning pace.

6. Break rhythms

I think that people who are long-distance runners have a different built-in rhythm than runners in sprint races. It's not just a matter of differences in their capacity for endurance vs. quick spurts. It's also a matter of the amount of time between breaks, meaning the break frequency, the break rhythm.

7. The nonrhythms of meetings

This will be my last example. Seven is a sacred number, so it's appropriate. And it's a counter-example: meetings. I've chosen this because it's one of the situations in which my sensitivity to experienced nonrhythms is the strongest. An assembly of people gathered for the purpose of airing a question in a more or less disciplined fashion (often less), from widely diverse viewpoints, and then making a decision—it's a process I find it almost impossible to participate in. In the past I would sit at the meeting and write letters or think new thoughts while trying to look alert. I can't do that anymore. Nowadays I get caught up in the meaninglessness of it, and it turns into a big mental nightmare.

I assume that I'm peculiar in this case, since the meeting format is so widespread. Other people clearly don't have the same resistance to letting the rhythm of their thoughts be shackled during meetings. So maybe it won't make much difference if I express strong objections here. But I'm still a little curious all the same: is it possible that there are people who are in tune with the rhythm of meetings? Or is it simply that they have less sensitivity and thus a higher tolerance for non-rhythms?

Chapter Nine

Forward and Backward Thoughts

There are two ways to answer the most common question: "Why?" One explains the background, the other the intention. This chapter deals with the difference in what we see if we proceed from the backward-looking "because of" or from the forward-looking "so that."

The idea that time has direction is also an important characteristic of time.

We live our lives moving forward. Our expectations point forward. As do our intentions. No one could even get up from his chair without having some intention—he would stay sitting there for all eternity, like a block of granite. Intentions, whether conscious or unconscious, are among the many characteristics that distinguish the living from the dead. The living possess innate and acquired intentions; the dead lack any intentions whatsoever. The only causal relationship that can be tracked is how the past has led to the present, not how the present points forward.

In education it's particularly important to look forward. It's strange that we so often concentrate on previous knowledge. Knowledge that precedes us is, of course, important, but it deals only with things as they once were. It's just as important to consider things that point forward: expectations, hopes, objectives.

The Teleological and the Mechanistic

I'll start with backward thinking, *the mechanistic approach*, which describes how events arise "because of." Science has been blamed for the idea that all humanity sees not only the universe but everything else as clockwork. And as clockwork, it's possible to refer everything to the past, to what is already built in.

Allow me first to say that it's unjust to accuse science of representing this point of view. It's one thing to show that physical consequences follow what we call natural laws, meaning human descriptions of the way "nature" functions. It's quite another matter to blame science for the spread of this point of view far beyond the realm of science. Scientists have played no part in this.

Physics has nothing to say about human beings and their biological capabilities, and it's not as a physicist that I've wondered, for instance, about human beings and memory. I'm not only a scientist—I'm also "a person who happens to be a scientist." It's from this perspective that I speculate here about memory and the consequences of various memory theories.

There are basically two theories about memory. One says that everything in memory remains unchanged. The other says that memory is constantly being reshaped. If you're an adherent of the first theory, it seems likely that an individual is always being guided (consciously or unconsciously) by his previous experiences. He is practically chained to them, without the possibility of fundamentally reassessing or erasing them. In that case, we may see our lives as being quite mechanistic: most things occur "because of" something and not as a result of any intentions we may have.

The second theory makes the claim that the past is continually being reshaped. This means that memory is not merely a contemporary record of events but also something that undergoes constant change.

The two different theories about memory are employed in parallel. When a psychologist serves as an expert witness, her conclusions will depend on which theory she advocates. If she believes that events remain intact, indelibly photographed as memory images, then a child's drawings and statements will be interpreted in one way. If she believes that memory images can be reshaped, the interpretation will be different. In legal situations, it would be sensible for the court to begin by establishing which fundamental memory theory the psychologist advocates. Only then should her expert testimony be considered.

Backward Thinking, for Better or Worse

To a large extent it's our experiences that shape us. Experiences are what give us associations, knowledge, and emotions. It's impossible to imagine a human being without backward thoughts; even a newborn has many experiences. Later in life, experiences are constantly present, and they have a great influence on our personality—in terms of both important and trivial matters.

Compare two people jumping from rock to rock

on the seashore. They choose different paths and they jump in completely different ways. With each jump our subconscious thoughts flash through a number of possibilities regarding choice of rock, how to place our feet, and speed. Most of the possibilities are rejected as our experience discards the less advantageous solutions. The combination of our individual perception of reality and our personal experience results in different choices and ways of jumping for different people. And we don't always make the same kinds of choices either. Which is as it should be. Individual development would come to a complete standstill if we didn't have an innate desire to try out new possibilities. It can't be emphasized enough that variation rather than repetition is the mother of all learning. But the old ways are also needed for the sake of variation, as something to inspire variation or as something to which the new can be compared.

But an insistence on backward thinking is definitely wrong if the situation is totally new and the old experience no longer applies. A small child who has no experience with brittle ice will unsuspectingly walk out onto thin ice. And a school that has no experience with the Internet and its impact on learning will unsuspectingly start off with the old student-teacher relationships.

Linear vs. Circular Thinking

Our culture is in every respect based on linear thinking. In this type of culture, it's understandably important to analyze the consequences of thinking forward as opposed to thinking backward. But if a culture has its roots in circular thinking, is it possible that direction is not as important? Let's take a brief look at the thought traditions of Greece vs. China.

Our culture has been strongly influenced by the Greek culture. In ancient Greece everything was once thought to consist of four elements: earth, water, air, and fire. These elements were partly associated with four properties: cold, wet, hot, and dry. And partly with the human body in terms of corresponding bodily fluids (black bile, phlegm, blood, yellow bile) and traits that signify character and temperament (melancholic, phlegmatic, sanguine, and choleric). It was essential to the whole structure of this model that the four elements were independent of each other and that they were in no way part of any hierarchy.

In China they happened to have five elements

(metal, wood, earth, water, and fire) instead of the four of the West. The five elements of the Chinese were dependent on each other. They were supposed to be arranged in the order given above—and preferably in a circle. Because 1) metal cuts 2) wood (with a piece of metal you can carve wood); wood cuts 3) earth (you can rake with a wooden rake); earth cuts 4) water (it can absorb water); water cuts 5) fire (water can extinguish fire). And to top it all off, the finishing touch is: fire cuts 1) metal, since fire can melt metal. With that the circle is closed.

It seems reasonable to transfer the difference between the Greek and Chinese ways of thinking (linear vs. circular) to the perception of time: as something that is either forward-moving or cyclical.

In our linear culture, the direction along the time axis has been displaced from the Greeks' forward-looking description of purposes to the contemporary emphasis on the cause that precedes the effect. If a small child in ancient Greece asked, "Why is there an acorn lying here?," the answer would have been, "An acorn is lying here so that it can grow up to be an oak tree." The Greeks had a teleological model for explaining things, that is, one based on an ultimate design or purpose. Nowadays, if you're outside with a child who wonders about the acorn, you'll reply, "Look up, honey! There's an oak tree here. The oak tree has dropped the acorn." In our mechanistic way of thinking, the cause has to come before the effect.

Few people have realized that technology, the driving force of our era, is based on a thought pattern that is exactly like the old teleological point of view. If someone makes a clock, it's done *so that* it will display the time. In a sense, the designer builds his purpose into the clock. Even though he can later apply the scientific explanatory model and say that the clock functions *because of* this or that reason, it won't alter the basic fact: he created the clock from a "so that" perspective.

What if we could learn differently by looking for purposes rather than just for causes? All new knowledge, from the outermost reaches of the universe down to the smallest detail of the microcosm, surprises us by pointing out how functional, how incomparably purposeful the design of nature appears to be. And yet we stubbornly refuse to search for knowledge structures based on purpose. Is this really sensible? Shouldn't we instead allow ourselves to strive for an economy of thought? And dare to admit that economical thoughts are pleasant to have and pleasant to live with? What if entirely different kinds of people were drawn to research with the "so that" mode than are drawn to research with the causal mode? Perhaps this could be something for women.

Forward Thoughts, Visions

Forward thoughts have a lot to do with having visions, inner images of how things could be, and then later attempts to realize them. When I saw a big Leonardo da Vinci exhibition recently, I spent most of my time walking around philosophizing. I thought about how much that man must have seen inside himself. The constant swarm of concrete internal images was probably the greatest and most important gift he had. Of course it was his extraordinary ability to draw and paint that made him well-known to his contemporaries and immortal to posterity. But for me, what was most remarkable about his rich paintings and immense productivity was the intensity, quantity, and degree of concreteness of his internal images, to which the outer pictures bear witness.

Those of us who are not visual artists also have inner pictures. We see them with varying degrees of clarity. We use them more or less consciously. What we have in common is that the inner pictures guide us. The more concrete the images and the more emotion-laden they are, the more powerful their influence. That's why it's unfortunate, to put it mildly, that most people and most systems seldom initially experience a good new idea as particularly concrete and thus influential.

On the other hand, we see concrete problems inside ourselves as soon as we imagine realizing an idea. And as if it weren't enough that the images of the problems are concrete, often they're also emotion-laden. This means that imagined problems can easily dominate our visions. People simply can't bring themselves to make their good, constructive thoughts as concrete and emotion-laden as the images of the problems. And so plenty of ideas are stifled in their infancy.

Backcasting

There may be a way to get around this, by turning back time through backcasting. Here goes: imagine how things will be in five years. Position yourself there, and then look back. Now try to figure out how you arrived there. Make a timetable, nail down intermediate goals, deadlines, before-and-after relationships, and so on. My experience in working as a manager, also within the field of science, is that many people have a remarkably difficult time making their visions concrete if they have to look ahead. But if they turn everything around by starting out guessing what it would be like to stand there in the future and look back in the rearview mirror, it works much better.

Many times I've wondered why this is easier, since it so obviously is. Perhaps it has to do with the way we use our memory. We think we know how we've arrived at the place where we now are. Analyzing backward is a well-known method. We can also use it successfully on the future. We just have to start by pretending that we're already there.

One of the many advantages with backcasting is that problems seen in the rearview mirror don't have nearly the overwhelming significance they might have when we look forward. In backcasting they become smaller. We see things in the rearview mirror the way we usually do when remembering. And our memory is not dominated by problems. On the contrary, many of us have recollections that diminish the problems which, in spite of everything, must have existed. A combination of problem-dominated visions and problem-reducing backcasting might give us a good and realistic perspective on the future.

We can draw inspiration from an argument of classical philosophy as we further ponder the advantages of backcasting. The argument has to do with plans for a military seizure of a foreign city. The discussion is directed at various ways for the army to make it over the city walls. Should they choose ladders, storm the walls, or create a blockade to starve the city's populace? Or should they shoot arrows? Or perhaps try to set the city on fire? The choice of an assault strategy seems to preoccupy all the thoughts of the attackers. Until someone steps forward and says, *What if we already had taken the city? Then what would we use it for?*

The answer to the question might be to decide not to attack at all. Or to adjust the method of attack to its long-term effects, seen in relation to why the attackers want the city.

My own interest in backcasting is directed at improving not military strategies but civilian ones. To achieve a specific goal, it pays to make an attempt to see with the eyes you imagine you might have after you've reached that goal.

Sacrifice on the Altar of Unreality

Everything I've said so far is based on the assumption that, either forward or backward, we need to think about the concrete, about what we can use in our external lives as a jumping-off point. If we think about something that isn't real, it presumably doesn't make any difference in which direction we try to look along the time axis.

Think of my feeling of unreality at the World's Fair in Lisbon, at Expo 98—was that a true indicator? There I had the sense of walking through an exhibit of brand names rather than products. As if it were primarily unreal things, abstractions, or symbols that were on display. Is that how far we've come?

Another thought along the same lines recently occurred to me when I compared our common environmental inheritance (earth, air, and water) to our common tele-culture inheritance (news media, electronic money, and the entertainment industry). It's the latter three that influence our thoughts every day; they have imperceptibly taken over our thoughts about the environment's atoms in the earth, air, and water. Whether or not the tele-culture is more important than our common environmental inheritance, information technology's part of the electromagnetic spectrum has become the most important natural resource of our age. It's symptomatic that this is not something visible. There is nothing that can be claimed through external gestures. The distribution is put into effect through international agreements, which are generally seen only in small articles in the newspapers.

In his book *The Little Prince*, the French author Antoine de Saint-Exupéry successfully expressed what links the past and the future most strongly. Here is an excerpt of the conversation between the Little Prince and the fox:

> "It's the time you spent on your rose that makes your rose so important."
>
> "It's the time I spent on my rose...," the little prince repeated, in order to remember.
>
> "People have forgotten this truth," the fox said. "But you mustn't forget it. You become responsible forever for what you're tamed. You're responsible for your rose..."
>
> "I'm responsible for my rose...," the little prince repeated, in order to remember.

Something or someone that you become attached to, something or someone that you "tame," whether in reality or not, is what will give you the strongest foothold in life. It's what gives you purpose and meaning—in both directions.

Chapter Ten

Why Are There
So Few Poodles?

Your perception of time is based on a few fundamental inner perceptions. Some of them may have changed by reading this book. If so, dare to allow the new ideas to affect your perception of the world. To help make this happen, and to make it possible for you to laugh a little at yourself, why not laugh at the way inner perceptions have ruled other people. Once more we turn to Greece and to the number ten.

This is the tenth and last chapter. And that's no coincidence. I planned it this way. Not just because we have ten fingers, ten toes, and a decimal system based on the number ten, but also because I wanted to talk about how the number ten was regarded in mystical numerology in Greece.

In ancient times, whole numbers had a special value, particularly the first ones:

1 stood for a point
2 stood for a line
3 stood for surface
4 stood for volume

That took care of all the available spatial dimensions (the dimension of time is not something that human beings really understand). If the numbers 1, 2, 3, and 4 were each considered sacred, then shouldn't the combination of these sacred numbers, their sum total, be even more sacred? What do $1 + 2 + 3 + 4$ add up to? Ten, of course.

Thus the number 10 became all-powerful for anything that was worth thinking about in ancient Greek times. For instance, when they were able to count nine unique heavenly phenomena (they liberally mixed together the sun and moon, the planets, and certain stars) but knew that there *had* to be ten, they were in big trouble. They came up with the counter earth, which was placed behind the sun. When the sun moved around the earth (which is what they then believed), the counter earth simultaneously moved on the other side of the sun.

In this way a truth was established that could be neither questioned nor checked—one of those dangerous truths. It was true because it had to be true. But notice that they didn't "invent" the counter earth. It was there because it had to be there.

It's the same thing with our society's perception that we "don't have enough time." The wisdom in the statement that we don't have enough time because we don't have enough time doesn't seem particularly overwhelming. But it has great power.

Perceptions of Time

Everyone has perceptions of how things must be. We prefer to think that things turn out the way they do because they have to. This book is a little circumspect because I *want* it to be that way. Maybe this circumspection is no less ridiculous than the rationalizations of the Greeks. By the way, it wouldn't be the worst thing if I at least managed to provoke a few good laughs. There's far too little laughter these days.

Laughter belongs on the list of activities that we humans need time for. In his "Basic Needs and Their Time," Guido Schwarz establishes eleven basic human needs. Among them are the types of activities that people must be allowed to carry out, needs that must be satisfied for an individual to survive. Think about whether the list below covers your basic needs or whether you would change anything:

Sleeping
Drinking
Eating
Using the toilet
Protecting yourself from heat, cold, wind
Having social contacts
Laughing
Having sexual contacts
Crying
Sinking into ecstasy
Cogitating

Parrots, Chameleons, and Poodles

A great deal is required to get away from habits based on segmented time. Or habits born from a feeling of constantly being chased by time, habits that might originate from a feeling of meaninglessness. I'll introduce here an inner menagerie that might be of some help. It has to do with parrots, chameleons, and poodles.

Let the parrot symbolize everything imitative that we humans are so often faced with and with which we surround ourselves. All those necessary (and quite ordinary) hoops we jump through to achieve a life of recognition. A calendar that is always jam-packed, time that is fragmented, a ringing telephone, a growing feeling of inadequacy.

Then equip yourself with a few chameleons. I mean the kind that are parrot-like (I know it's a big stretch), but that have perhaps—literally—changed color and assumed a different guise. In the chameleon world it's allowable, for instance, to take into consideration setup time and undivided time. In this way you only have to make sure that the sum of activities carried out is the same. This is already a big step forward, and it should make you feel a lot better.

Finally, you should breed a few poodles. They represent your efforts that are directed at what is at the core of the poodle. By this I mean trying to find what lies behind, touching on your innermost dreams, looking past all obstructive facades. There may be a shortage of poodles precisely because it's so hard to come up with innovations. It's hard to free yourself from the way other people do things, to make yourself think genuinely new thoughts. Sometimes I think that poodles are especially rare in the context of time. It's precisely

Thoughts about Time that take the most time to rejuvenate.

If you happen to have a flash of genius, find a core, and turn into a poodle, it's not guaranteed that you'll dare to talk about your new idea or that the rest of the world will permit you to realize it. There's a whole series of obstacles, but the worst is usually the fear of what's different. There may also be a lack of understanding: something new simply doesn't fit into the old worldview. That's why we don't want to see what's new; the person with new ideas may even be accused of doing things the wrong way.

Sometimes the repudiation of what's new is hidden behind the great "everyone" threat: "What would happen if *everyone* did that?!" Then you should simply reply, "Don't worry, it would be just fine, because for one thing, everyone *wouldn't* do that!" There's little risk that the poodles will end up dominating the parrots and the chameleons. Instead, the poodles are so threatened by extinction from the moment they're born that vigorous groups of poodles have trouble finding peace to develop.

One important factor hindering poodles is a widespread pessimism about the future. And certainly if there's not going to be any future, why should you come up with anything new?

Parrots and Quick Imitation

Western pessimism about the future can seem to absolve us of our obligations. This gloomy outlook may in many ways be well-founded, but the most important aspect is often missed: the human being himself. The idea that humans can take action isn't considered. And furthermore:

> Optimism is by its nature
> not a goal for the present situation
> but a life-force,
> a force for hope when others give up,
> a force for withstanding setbacks,
> a force that never surrenders the future to
> pessimism
> but rather requisitions it for hope.

This is what the theologian Dietrich Bonhoeffer (1906–1945) wrote as he sat in a concentration camp, awaiting execution.

How serious an effect your pessimism about the future will have on other people depends on your profession, among other things. A teacher who no longer believes in the future should seriously consider resigning. It seems unlikely that you could work in a school, which by definition is directed toward the future, if you yourself are pessimistic about the future. Spreading mental corrosion among children should be regarded as a breach of duty.

There's a classic expression that it doesn't befit a human being to give up. The idea can be expressed even more strongly: it's actually not human to give up. A human being is not made that way. Imagine someone who can't swim who ends up in deep water. It's not very common, even in a thought experiment, for the person in question to say, "I can't swim, so I might as well drown." No, he paddles around as best he can. He might even paddle harder, the poorer his ability to swim. And maybe he survives, maybe he doesn't. But he doesn't just give up because it looks like his chances have been exhausted.

The future is not some mountainside we're all going to smash into. Nor is it some kind of precipice and we're all going to fall off the edge. We'll do what people have always done: we'll try.

If you too carry this insight, then guard it well. It's a prerequisite for good thoughts about time. Don't get too upset if you encounter opposition.

It's not so easy for other people to relate to you as a poodle if they've only met parrots before.

What I Wonder About

In the preface I wrote that I've been dealing with much of the contents of this book for more than twenty years. If I now instead look ahead twenty years, what is that I would have liked to know? For every idea that I've described in this book, new thoughts have occurred to me. The strongest of them is the most challenging: how will the number of sweeping changes during a lifetime have changed? (I know that it won't be an entire lifetime for me until the year 2019, but it's the trend that I'm interested in.)

A human being is (for himself) the measure of all things. The length of a human life is thus guaranteed to be *one* measure. The continuous rate of change that a person can accept is another measure. But the rate of change doesn't always have the effect you think.

A banal example: if the number of lunch choices is increased from 10 to 1,000, this won't have much impact on you. You demonstrate that you're the measure of all things by the fact that you still can't eat more than one lunch per day. But the extent of the lunch menu, like all other expanding multiplicities, causes you to have even more opportunities to distinguish yourself from those around you. This affects (for better or worse) external social interaction.

But more important, I think, is a person's *internal* social interaction. Your imprinting and re-imprinting may constantly give you new standards for measuring new ideas. But can a generation handle an unspecified number of imprintings of unspecified strength? Will people end up, for instance, aging faster in years to come, out of absolute necessity? Should a human life actually be shorter in order to correspond to a reasonable number of changes occurring during a lifetime?

There's nothing that says the rate of development should be constant, meaning that two changes in 1999 should be followed by two changes in 2000, and so on, making a total of forty changes by the year 2019.

No, it looks more as if a doubling of the rate of change in 1999 would yield another doubling in the year 2000 (i.e., a factor of four), then an eight-fold increase in 2001, a sixteen-fold increase in 2002...Go ahead and calculate what this would mean for the year 2019. You'll come up with an absurdly big number.

I don't *think* that the number of sweeping

changes during a human lifetime will end up esca-
lating in this way (or even that changes can be cal-
culated in "pieces"). At the same time, I can't see
what would prevent these artificial exponential
functions from ticking away. That's why I let myself wonder. And that's why I let myself believe
that it's important for many more people to give a
lot more thought to their relationship to time.